THE PEOPLE V. HARVARD LAW

THE PEOPLE V. HARVARD LAW

HOW AMERICA'S OLDEST LAW SCHOOL TURNED ITS BACK ON FREE SPEECH

ANDREW PEYTON THOMAS

ENCOUNTER BOOKS
SAN FRANCISCO

First edition published in 2005 by Encounter Books, an activity of Encounter for Culture and Education, Inc., a nonprofit corporation.

Encounter Books website address: www.encounterbooks.com

Manufactured in the United States and printed on acid-free paper.

The paper used in this publication meets the minimum requirements of ANSI/NISO Z39.48-1992 (R 1997)(*Permanence of Paper*).

FIRST EDITION

Library of Congress Cataloging-in-Publication Data

Thomas, Andrew Peyton.
    The People v. Harvard Law : how America's oldest law school turned its back on free speech / Andrew Peyton Thomas.
        p. cm.
    Includes bibliographical references and index.
    ISBN 1-893554-98-8 (alk. paper)
    1. Harvard Law School.   2. Law schools—Political aspect—Massachusetts—Cambridge.   3. Freedom of speech—Massachusetts—Cambridge.   4. Political correctness—Massachusetts—Cambridge.
    I. Title.
    KF292.H3 T48 2005
    340'.071'17444—dc22   2004065020

10 9 8 7 6 5 4 3 2 1

For Jackson, and for my parents

CONTENTS

1   Prologue: Property Crimes

31   Chapter One: Crocodile Hunting

47   Chapter Two: Up in Smoke

57   Chapter Three: The Limits of Tenure

65   Chapter Four: Boneless Bob

91   Chapter Five: Triumph of the Crits

103   Chapter Six: Diversity, Harvard Style

117   Chapter Seven: "Conservatives Should Shut Up about Silencing"

135   Chapter Eight: Poetic Injustice

145   Chapter Nine: The Socratic Method Becomes a Hate Crime

159   Chapter Ten: Worlds Apart

169   Chapter Eleven: Un-Martial Law

179   Chapter Twelve: Breaking the Code

197   Acknowledgments

199   Notes

211   Index

PROPERTY CRIMES

FEW WHO KNEW KIWI CAMARA in his hometown of Honolulu were surprised when he gained admission to Harvard. Anything less for this prodigy would have meant underachievement. The only child of two physicians, both Filipino-Americans, Camara had pursued outsized dreams from a young age. Both parental and personal ambition fueled him as he rocketed through the traditional levels of elementary and secondary education. A high score on the SAT in the seventh grade punched Camara's ticket to higher education; he opted to skip junior high and high school and enrolled instead at a local college. He took courses year round, forgoing any summer indulgence in the many distractions of the tropical paradise around him. His natural gifts and his dogged self-denial bore fruit early, as Camara earned his bachelor's degree in computer science at Hawaii Pacific University at the age of fifteen.

With a cornucopia of professional options before him, Camara decided on a career in law. In 2000, he applied to law schools across the country, with Harvard at the top of his wish list. The nation's oldest law school, Harvard had become, in its almost two centuries of existence, a foundry of leading attorneys, professors, politicians, judges and other people of prominence throughout American society. Although it was the most prestigious law school in the country, Harvard Law admitted more students per year than other preeminent schools— over five hundred students per class, or more than three times as many students as, for example, Yale or Stanford. This differential actually made Harvard somewhat less exclusive than these other top schools, yet its sheer numerical advantage helped make Harvard number one. As more Harvard graduates went forth into the world every year, it was more likely, as a matter of simple mathematics, that they would end up disproportionately at the pinnacle of their professions. This bolstered Harvard's reputation, and year after year the school attracted talented young people like Kiwi Camara.

By the time Robert Clark, dean of Harvard Law School, flew to Honolulu in 2000 for a fundraising trip, Camara had already become a minor celebrity on the islands. Honolulu's major newspaper helpfully advertised for Camara by splashing on its pages, the very day of Clark's arrival, an article about the local wonder-boy. When they met that day, Clark and Camara bóth seemed excited by the prospect of Camara's attending Harvard Law.

Camara arrived in Cambridge, Massachusetts, in the fall of 2001 as the youngest student in the history of the law school. He was sixteen, barely old enough to obtain a driver's license. Camara (and, for that matter, his parents) would learn there was a downside to moving an intellectually gifted child through the educational system at warp speed. In Camara's case, it would prove a staggering cost, one that would nullify, in one ill-advised act, all his prior achievements and sacrifices.

Camara adapted simultaneously to the wintry northern climate and to academic competition far beyond anything he had previously experienced. He followed the well-trod path to success at Harvard: reading and parsing the assigned cases prior to class, attending classes faithfully, taking copious notes, writing course outlines. Before sitting for examinations, he studied his notes and outlines until he absorbed everything from basic principles of law to the relatively minor legal arcana of interest only to his professors.

After taking exams for his fall semester classes, Camara, like his classmates, no longer had much use for his class notes and outlines. He gave them little thought until he received a blast e-mail from the law school's Web site, HLCentral. The Web site asked the first-year students—or 1Ls, as they were called—to donate their class outlines to this online information bank. The Web site was to serve as a clearinghouse of class notes for future 1Ls as well as an archive of interest to legal historians (many of Camara's classmates were presumably destined for leading careers in law and society). HLCentral informed the students that the outlines would be posted and available online to all members of the law school community.

Camara saw no harm in sending his outlines to HLCentral. He had no doubt that others would benefit from them. (Already, his classmates regarded Camara as an oddball with an ego in proportion to his giant youthful accomplishments.) He filled out the electronic form accompanying the e-mail and attached his outlines. On February 18, 2002, he clicked on the HLCentral link and transmitted his work to the online bank.

This would prove to be a profound mistake, one that would trigger a cataclysm for Camara personally and a crisis for the law school.

Both his decision to post his outlines and the contents of the outlines themselves reflected, among other things, immaturity—a quality painfully obvious to all who observed this teenager studying and competing among young adults. To some of his classmates, Camara's callowness was evident in an odd and unseemly brashness, something out of place at Harvard. While the law school was a notorious playground for egotists, it was also an institution in which, by an unwritten code, past or present achievements were almost never spoken of. All members of the community were presumed to be there for good reason; the assumption was that they would let their achievements at the school do the talking for them. Camara brazenly flouted these rules.

Other students, speaking of his immaturity, were quick to mention the personal Web site that Camara maintained. It featured Camara singing a silly song and offering fashion tips.

But if it had merely been a case of juvenile behavior, Camara would have been considered an eccentric. The problem—for him and for Harvard too, as it worked out—was that in the course outlines Camara had submitted to the online bank, he had used a truncated racial slur as an abbreviation for African-Americans. He employed this device in his outline for property class, and in particular his discussion of *Shelley v. Kraemer.* In the landmark 1948 case, the Supreme Court struck down racially restrictive covenants, or provisions in real estate contracts designed to exclude racial minorities from certain neighborhoods. In his notes, Camara summarized the central issue as: "Nigs buy land w/ no nig covenant; Q: Enforceable?"

It was bad enough that Camara had used slurs in his notes and then posted them on a communal Web site. Even more stunning and peculiar was the disclaimer that he attached to his outlines. He explicitly warned prospective readers that he had used "offensive racial shorthand" in taking class notes. When asked why, if he knew they were offensive, he did not remove such comments before submitting his outlines for public inspection, Camara later responded that he "didn't want to rummage through 150 pages of notes and make them politically correct."

Almost a month passed before anybody clicked through the class outlines and detonated the time bomb that Camara had planted there. Then one of Camara's African-American classmates from Section IV viewed his offering and was outraged. F. Michelle Simpson was known to her classmates primarily for her physical attractiveness and outspokenness. A native of Nashville, Tennessee, Simpson had graduated from Howard University before seeking her law degree. She was direct and free-spoken in class, and made a striking impression because of her combination of good looks and assertiveness. Like the vast majority in the sea of students sitting around her, she was left-leaning in her politics.

On March 7, Simpson complained to the law school's webmaster about the language she had discovered in Camara's notes. "If a person feels a certain way towards a group," she wrote, "and the 1st amendment gives him the right to express those views, please don't allow your helpful public study tool to be used by that person to degrade that group." Even as she acknowledged Camara's right to make such statements, Simpson would press the powers-that-be at Harvard to scrub them from the Web site. It was not the last time such philosophical contradictions would arise in a discussion of Camara's notes.

After being informed of the complaint, Camara, duly abashed, promptly took down his outlines. He assumed the matter would end there. He obviously did not know Simpson—or Harvard Law—very well.

He would learn in short order that things were not so simple at this school, whose political and ideological undercurrents were as treacherous as any in American higher education.

By virtue of its unique history and status, Harvard had become, by the time Camara enrolled, a prime battlefield for those who recognized the power of law to reshape the American nation. He would soon be another casualty in the intellectual cold war that had been raging in Cambridge long before he arrived and would continue to cause collateral damage long after he was gone.

BY THE TIME CAMARA POSTED his toxic class notes, Harvard Law was approaching its two hundredth birthday. The law school was about half as old as Harvard University itself. That Harvard had lacked a law school for almost half its existence was not for lack of interest in law. The university's original library had housed works on law beginning in 1638. The school's founder, John Harvard, personally donated a number of them, such as the 1587 edition of *The whole volume of statutes at large ... since Magna Carta until the 29th yeere of Ladie Elizabeth.* While the main preoccupation of the early Puritan masters of Harvard was preparing students for the ministry, law provided the necessary undergirding for a civil society in which faith could be practiced freely. It was never far from the Puritan mind.

But it was not until the mid-eighteenth century that law gained acceptance as a discrete discipline worthy of formal study at a university. The main force behind this change was William Blackstone. A professor at Oxford, Blackstone tried to teach undergraduates some basic knowledge of law as part of their core curriculum. He explained, "I think it an undeniable position that a competent knowledge of the laws of that society, in which we live, is the proper accomplishment of every gentleman and scholar; a highly useful, I had almost said essential, part of liberal and polite education." In 1756, Oxford designated Blackstone as a professor of common law studies, making him the first law professor ever. His lectures were published as *Commentaries on the Laws of England,* of which 2,500 copies were sold in America prior to the Constitutional Convention in 1787.

Blackstone's innovations in legal pedagogy also traveled to America. In 1779, William and Mary College established the first professorship of law. Thomas Jefferson became a Visitor at the school in the same year he became governor of Virginia, and set up a chair of "law and police" as part of his program of instruction. Following the American Revolution, a loyalist who had fled his native Massachusetts after the initial crackling of musketry would provide Harvard with its first law professorship. In his will, Isaac Royall endowed Harvard with "a Professor of Laws in said College or a Professor of Physick and Anatomy." Following Royall's death in England in 1781, Harvard found that the local patriots had confiscated much of his real estate during his absence; the college resorted to litigating its claims in court. It would not be the last time that Harvard would look to the courts to extend its influence.

After winning its claims to Royall's contested land, Harvard sold off parcels over the years to finance its growth. The proceeds were used to underwrite investments in land and buildings contiguous to the original site of the college, which was located along the banks of the Charles River in Cambridge, five miles west of Boston. These swelling funds also paid for staff expenses, but it was not until 1815 that Harvard finally appointed its first professor of law. One historian noted that this was 95 years after the college established a chair of divinity, 33 years after it created its first professorship of medicine, and 34 years after Royall's death. The leaders of Harvard were not in a hurry to promote legal education because other intellectual pursuits seemed more imperative and because there did not seem to be much demand. Indeed, even many aspiring attorneys still believed that law was not something that required formal classroom instruction. Just as new schools of business would later be greeted with skepticism, law schools were regarded by attorneys and academics alike as an inessential novelty. Law, they believed, was best learned through practice in the rough-and-tumble of the real world.

Two more years passed before Harvard Law School came into existence. Finally, in 1817, Harvard's Board of Overseers voted to establish "a school for the instruction of students at law, at Cambridge, under the patronage of the University." Six students enrolled in the first year. Students did not stay for a three-year program of study, as they would in later years, but only until they felt sufficiently conversant with the law to be able to obtain a license to practice. For these first students, the purpose of a legal education was not to ruminate on legal theory, but merely to move into their careers more quickly.

This conception began to change in 1828, when Harvard invited a justice of the U.S. Supreme Court, Joseph Story, to become a professor at the law school. A denizen of Salem, Massachusetts, Story was a prolific writer as well as an esteemed jurist, and had already written several seminal books on law. Harvard met his terms, which meant accommodating the Renaissance man so that Story could continue to sit on the high court. He would spend the winter and early spring on the Supreme Court bench in Washington, and while at Harvard for the rest of the year he would traverse New England as the circuit justice for federal courts in the region. Story's multiple accomplishments—service on the high court, publication of his great work *Commentaries on the Constitution,* and delivery of thoughtful lectures as a professor—solidified Harvard Law's status as the nation's leading law school.

When young Oliver Wendell Holmes enrolled in September 1829, he wrote to a friend that he had "settled once more" amid "Blackstone and boots, law and lathe, Rawle and rasps, all intermingled in exquisite confusion." Holmes added, "... I thought of going away to study my profession but since Judge Story and Mr. Ashmun [another professor] have come, the Law School is so flourishing that I have thought it best to stay where I am." It was good for both man and school that he stayed: Holmes became a lecturer on jurisprudence at Harvard in 1871 and a full professor of law in 1882, and ultimately one of its most illustrious graduates. In remarks to the Harvard Law School Association in 1886, he reflected on the proper mission of the institution. He stated, "The aim of a law school should be, the aim of the Harvard Law School has been, not to make men smart but to make them wise in their calling— to start them on a road which will lead them to the abode of the masters. A law school should be at once the workshop and the nursery of specialists." Holmes would become a Supreme Court justice whose fame would rival that of Story. He led a parade of other great professors and jurists who followed him at Harvard: Louis Brandeis, Roscoe Pound, Felix Frankfurter.

An important part of Harvard's continuing success was its balance of rigor and creativity in the classroom. In the 1950s, Professor Edward H. "Bull" Warren would rattle his first-year students by openly predicting that one out of three of them would fail to graduate. "Look to the left, look to the right, look at yourself," he would bark. "One of you three won't be here next year." And yet the school was also a cradle of inventive pedagogy.

Harvard fathered innovations in teaching that revolution-
ized the study of law. The most far-reaching of these were the
case-study and the Socratic methods of instruction. Dean
Christopher Columbus Langdell initiated the case-study method
in the late 1800s. He believed that students should not simply
learn the fundamental principles of law by rote. Instead, they
should be encouraged to study and compare different court
opinions and extract from these cases both the rulings and the
reasoning behind them. As part of this regimen, professors would
question students in class about the cases so the applicable principles of law could be fleshed out and debated. This mode of
questioning was styled the Socratic method, after the manner
in which the Athenian philosopher Socrates questioned his fol-
lowers in steering them toward discovery of the truth.

The case-study method, though resisted in Langdell's
time, became a cornerstone of accepted pedagogy at Harvard
and, subsequently, the nation's other law schools. This form of
teaching became famous through the influence of films such
as *The Paper Chase,* in which a glowering Professor Kingsfield
mercilessly grills his first-year students at Harvard. To aid in
conducting such questioning, professors often used seating
charts with photos from first-year student handbooks pasted
under the names, a practice that permitted easier identifica-
tion of the instructor's daily targets. Novelist Scott Turow, a
graduate of Harvard Law School, would write of the experience and remember the mixture of fear, uncertainty and pride
that drove students to prepare so thoroughly for class. "Some
[professors] interrogate students for thirty seconds—others
leave them on the hot seat for the entire class. . . . You are in
front of 140 people whom you respect, and you would like
them to think well of you." Those who came to class unprepared often would try "backbenching," or hiding in the back

of the classroom out of their assigned seats. Sometimes this worked; often the slackers were spotted and embarrassed.

These rigors had a purpose. Harvard Law gave diplomas with real meaning, diplomas that were the capstone of an education grounded in the rudiments of legal doctrine and seasoned with exposure to the newest ideas and trends in legal theory.

The intellectual fortunes of Harvard Law School would largely mirror the drift in American legal philosophy during the school's two hundred years of operation. Harvard Law was founded when natural law theory still dominated the Western legal mind. This theory, espoused most famously and successfully by Thomas Aquinas, held that law, properly defined, was a set of rules that applied the natural laws ordained by God to specific human conduct. Human laws that contravened natural law were, by Aquinas's reasoning, not morally binding on a citizen. Mahatma Gandhi and Martin Luther King invoked this theory of natural law to justify civil disobedience of laws they judged morally repugnant.

In the early nineteenth century, as Harvard Law set down its roots, another legal philosophy emerged from Great Britain to displace natural law theory: legal positivism. Coined by John Austin, legal positivism severed legality from morality. Austin defined law as a command issued by a sovereign, or a governmental entity capable of enforcing its laws successfully. For purposes of determining whether a rule was a law, Austin argued, it did not matter whether the rule was moral or immoral. What mattered was whether there was a government willing and able to make sure the people generally obeyed the rule. Critics of the theory noted that legal positivism rendered law indistinguishable from the demands of a gunman. But legal positivists argued that this definition of law was far more conducive to legal education—the basic process of identifying and studying laws—than one steeped in traditional moral precepts that made such classification more difficult.

Oliver Wendell Holmes became the leading exponent of the next major legal philosophy to hold sway in American law. Legal realism, which arose in the late 1800s, took legal positivism to another level by framing law from the perspective of the "bad man." This school of thought held that a law is a rule which, when violated, prompts the government to take action against the violator. The object of legal education, by the same token, is to try to predict under what circumstances the power of the state will be brought to bear against human behavior. Holmes and others of this school also disputed the view that the law consisted of discrete rules and precedents. Rather, they regarded the law as a compilation of decisions by those interpreting the rules; accordingly, the best way to predict the outcome of a case before a court of law was to study the pattern of decisions emanating from that court. Like legal positivism, legal realism divorced law from ethics.

Throughout most of the twentieth century, legal realism was the governing philosophy of Harvard Law School. Holmes and Dean Roscoe Pound, both products of Harvard Law, were the most famous advocates of applying these literally demoralizing theories to American law. By stripping law down to such basics, they believed, lawyers and law students would rightly perceive that statutes and court rulings inevitably reflected the personal values of the politicians, rulers and judges handing them down. Legal education would gain from studying the law in these more sober terms.

Yet such a cynical view of law was bound to bear unexpected and unfortunate fruit. By the latter part of the twentieth century, legal realism came under attack from the left as too stodgy and bourgeois. Beginning in the late 1970s, an off-shoot of Marxism known as Critical Legal Studies began to take hold and apply yet another analytical razor to law. Born in May 1977 at a law and society colloquium at Madison, Wisconsin, Critical Legal Studies was an outgrowth of the presumptuously named branch of philosophy known as postmodernism. This school of thought held that the central project of philosophy, properly understood, is to "deconstruct" language; and the inevitable result of such deconstruction is to lay waste to existing political and social institutions. The main figure in this line of analysis was the French philosopher Jacques Derrida, whose work was devoted to demonstrating the indeterminacy of language. Derrida and Michel Foucault argued that reality itself is essentially incomprehensible, and that human institutions reflect simply the preferences of the powerful. Postmodernism traced its lineage back to the earlier French philosophy of existentialism and ultimately to the philosophy of Jean-Jacques Rousseau, who advocated the primacy of sentiment and emotion over reason.

The "Crits," as such theorists became known, applied postmodernism to law. In their hands, law would become an instrument of social reconstruction, sweeping aside the corrupt societal infrastructure built by power groups—namely, white males. Crits were better levelers than architects, however, as they never quite made clear what they proposed to take the place of the legal structure they sought to tear down. The replacement regime they seemed to favor was whatever variant of interest-group liberalism happened to be the trend of the day. Critical Legal Studies was in reality a theoretical wrecking ball that slammed against American law and left behind the rubble of barren nihilism.

To the Crits, all law was a sham, and the law taught at Harvard only promoted the interests of the elite. The Crits argued that the wealthy and powerful manipulated the law to exploit the poor and retain power, and that any attempts to come up with objective legal principles conducive to a system of justice were humbug. Whoever controlled the law controlled society, the Crits noted, and they did their best to control the law where it counted most: the academy and the courts.

One of their main tactics was building up cadres of supporters in academia. From its inception, Critical Legal Studies became a cause as much as a legal theory. That the leaders of Critical Legal Studies flocked to Harvard Law School made good sense, as the school offered an attractive stage for advocates of this new philosophy. The first scholar of note in this strain was Roberto Unger. Born in 1947 in Brazil, Unger authored writings that reflected his roots in Latin America and a debt to liberation theology, the theory of violent class warfare invoked by Marxist guerrilla movements from El Salvador to Peru. From his tenured position at Harvard, Unger would apply these principles—minus the explicit calls for violence—to American law.

Unger viewed Critical Legal Studies not as an abstract theory but as a "program" or movement. More to the point, Critical Legal Studies was a kind of "superliberalism." Unger explained that Critical Legal Studies "pushes the liberal premises ... to the point at which they merge into a large ambition: the building of a social world less alien to a self that can always violate the generative rules of its own mental or social constructs and put other rules and other constructs in their place." By this he meant that Critical Legal Studies would wipe out the existing "metaorder," or politico-legal structure of the nation, and replace it with a Marxist philosophical and ethical system in which there were no clear rules of right and wrong, only an amorphous dedication to class warfare.

Unger acknowledged that this grand demolition may seem "an act of intellectual self-destruction." But good things would come of the annihilation. Unger argued that "this apparent intellectual suicide allows the basic intention and method of critical social thought to triumph over ideas that only imperfectly apply the method and express the intention."

How to implement this radical program? Unger thought the natural wellspring of intellectual revolution was academia. "The most immediate setting of our transformative activity is also on its face the most modest: the law schools," he explained. For students, "coming to law school often means putting aside in the name of reality an adolescent fantasy of social reconstruction or intellectual creation." This idealism can be molded into something more meaningful, even among students whose drive to succeed at law school is primarily financial. Unger's pragmatism was straightforward: "We build with what we have and willingly pay the price for the inconformity of vision to circumstance."

Students graduating with such a Crit-inspired, subversive mindset would then carry it out into the world. For this "program" to succeed, the practice of law should not be regarded as representing clients, even though the prevailing rules of legal ethics mandated this understanding. Instead, "For us, law practice should be, and to some extent always is, the legal defense of individual or group interests by methods that reveal the specificity of the underlying institutional and imaginative order, that subject it to a series of petty disturbances capable of escalating at any moment, and that suggest alternative ways of defining collective interests, collective identities, and assumptions about the possible." Attorneys, in short, should be agents of leftist social change rather than advocates for the individuals or businesses that hire them.

Unger's seminal theories offered notions of class struggle and interest-group politics that would hold sway over much
of the American legal intelligentsia at the turn of the twenty-
first century. Another important figure in the history of Critical Legal Studies, one who would apply these principles in even
less orthodox ways, was Duncan Kennedy, one of Unger's fellow professors at Harvard. Nicknamed "Funky Dunc,"
Kennedy was a tall man who cut a striking figure with his thin-
ning hair, shaggy beard, and faded denim jacket. His father
had been an architect in Cambridge and a professor at the
Massachusetts Institute of Technology; his mother was a poet.
Raised a child of academia, Kennedy recalled that his parents
"socialized me into the tradition of revolt against bourgeois
repression and into the cult of formal innovation, rather than
into the tradition of political radicalism. The keys were yearn-
ing ... originality ... the artist."

After graduating from Yale Law School, Kennedy clerked
for Justice Potter Stewart, then worked for a time as an associate at a prestigious firm in New York. But he never bothered
to take the bar exam, and later turned his back altogether on
the nonacademic world by returning to his hometown and joining the faculty at Harvard Law. Perhaps because of unpleasant experiences in corporate law, Kennedy later would urge
new lawyers to undermine the "hierarchy" at large law firms
by refusing, for example, to laugh at a partner's jokes. A con-
firmed eccentric, he eventually married a Boston socialite
named Mopsie Strange Kennedy; they and their two children,
Fifi and Kiki, resided in a Victorian mansion not far from the
law school.

Affectionately described by one Crit as "a cross between
Rasputin and Billy Graham," Duncan Kennedy made an
impression on the students and faculty of Harvard with his

unusual attire and behavior and the forthrightness of his far-left beliefs. He described communists, for example, as a "victim group," and in fact "the most 'like us' of victim groups"—"us" meaning Crits. African-Americans and poor people could not be held accountable for much if any wrongdoing; they "deserved unlimited sympathy and unquestioning respect because their lives were harder than ours and because many people other than ourselves were prejudiced against them." Like other Crits, he saw the practice of law as affording an opportunity to do more than resolve legal disputes with reasonable justice. The law exists "to secure both particular ideological and general class interests of the intelligentsia in the social and economic status quo." Ironically, however, by the time Kennedy penned these words, the critique he offered had turned in upon itself: The success of the Crits' project had ensured that the "ideological and general class interests" being championed by the legal "intelligentsia" were in no small measure the values of Critical Legal Studies.

Even by the standards of cloistered higher education, many of Kennedy's writings and theories were odd. His most famous law-review article was "Roll Over Beethoven," co-authored with another Crit, Peter Gabel. The article, published in 1984 in the *Stanford Law Review,* is essentially a rap session between two Crits who toss postmodern terminology back and forth in an exchange that is barely intelligible. A critic in the *Michigan Law Review* justly described the work as sounding like "a pair of old acid-heads chewing over a passage from Sartre."

Kennedy and Gabel argue in abstruse language over whether concepts such as love and rights are possible or comprehensible given the limits of language and logic. "Let's just call it love," Kennedy says at one point in an attempt to label the emotion. "I mean we can call it love this week and next week we'll call it community, and the week after that ..." The volleys continue:

> *Peter:* It depends on the context you're in whether you call it unalienated relatedness or ...
> *Duncan:* Sometimes it sounds like, "All these things can be reduced to the single master concept of unalienated relatedness that is immanent in our current situation." So that that formula would then be the privileged formula.
> *Peter:* It's not privileged. It's just a philosophical mode of getting at it.
> *Duncan:* Why can't I just call it yearning? What's wrong with calling it intersubjective zap? Or making the kettle boil? What's wrong with calling it ...

As they dispose of the concept of love, so go other cherished notions. The essential point of the colloquy, as with Critical Legal Studies generally, is to deconstruct language and concepts to the point that everything appears meaningless, and law professors are left to instruct the world on how to reshape the mess that remains.

Kennedy encouraged this nascent movement with quirky gimmicks and proposals. He proposed, for example, that a lottery be used to determine both admission to Harvard Law and selection for the prestigious law review (but, of course, not for faculty hiring). He also advocated that the law school pay professors and custodians the same wage, and even require professors and custodians to switch jobs from time to time. One impertinent student actually went to the trouble—apparently unlike Kennedy—of asking the janitors what they thought of the idea. Their responses were withering:

- "The only thing worse than scrubbing a toilet would be to have to pretend to be some fancy-pants, egghead college professor, usually some dweeby guy who couldn't do anything well but read books."
- "Tell this professor of yours to mind his own damn business! The world would be a lot better off without some screwed up, overeducated college brat telling the rest of us how to live our lives."
- "Maybe he can sell that line to a bunch of fruitcake students, but he sure can't fool us janitors."

When the student, Brian Timmons, published the results of this informal survey in the *Wall Street Journal* and reported the additional fact that this professor-of-the-proletariat drove a Jaguar to school, Kennedy cornered the young scribe and complained angrily that the Jaguar belonged to his wife.

A third important figure in Critical Legal Studies taught alongside Unger and Kennedy at Harvard. Morton Horwitz was best known among legal academicians as the author of the legal-historical work *The Transformation of American Law*. This critique of American legal traditions argued that nineteenth-century judges had engaged in judicial activism from the right, which "enabled emergent entrepreneurial and commercial groups to win a disproportionate share of wealth and power in American society." Through these right-wing judicial efforts, "the ideologies of laissez-faire and rugged individualism had finally established a prominent beachhead in American property doctrine."

Yet Horwitz's criticism of judicial activism was highly selective. In other writings, he took a very different view of judicial activism—as long as the activism in question was left of center. He devoted one book to lauding Chief Justice Earl Warren and Justice William Brennan for inaugurating the modern era of liberal judicial activism. Like virtually all professors at Harvard, Horwitz viewed Brennan, a Harvard graduate, as the archetypal modern justice, "one of the greatest justices in the nation's history." Horwitz expressed the conventional wisdom among Harvard Law professors when he hailed the Warren-Brennan axis for remaking the nation through judicial decree.

While Warren conferred his name on the activist Supreme Court that remade American society in the 1960s and 1970s, Horwitz noted, many of the most important opinions were Brennan's intellectual handiwork. Brennan had spurred the Court to make welfare a constitutionally protected property right. He had also urged the Court to abolish capital punishment, make abortion a constitutional right, increase the rights of prisoners and criminal defendants, and defend racial quotas. Almost all these rulings required an overturning of democratically enacted laws. Horwitz cheered the Warren-Brennan partnership for "redefining democracy" in a way less beholden to the will of the majority, and more in keeping with the prevailing values of the legal academy. In contrast, Horwitz wrote, the "Federalist understanding" of the Constitution "has developed into a cartoon" that does not focus sufficiently on "the centrality of minority rights."

As Horwitz's writings made clear, the Crits of Harvard Law believed that for all the unprecedented judicial activism of the preceding forty years, the courts still had not gone far enough. These "guerrillas with tenure," in Kennedy's memorable words, hoped that by expanding their influence in the nation's law schools, they could prod both academia and, inevitably, the courts further to the left. Toward this end, the Crits fought to admit more students with activist backgrounds and to hire more Crit professors. Fierce battles over faculty appointments were the result, arising regularly in the late 1980s and throughout the 1990s. From 1981 to 1985, Harvard Law did not appoint a single new professor to its faculty who was applying from another school—either because the faculty could not agree on a candidate or, when they did reach such a "Missouri Compromise," the professor spurned the offer from the embattled school.

The resulting chaos was helpful to the Crits. It drew attention to their cause, and even scared off at least one traditionalist professor, Paul Bator, a former deputy solicitor general in the Reagan administration, who fled to the University of Chicago. Duncan Kennedy and other Crits also urged the faithful to colonize other law schools with Crits to extend the empire. By 2002, the Crits had earned a place in Harvard Law's power structure similar to that of the Green Party in Germany: a far-left fringe group that, having acquired a certain base and respectability, had settled in and earned acceptance as an essential player in major decisions at the school.

Critical Legal Studies also spawned subsidiary movements that were just as influential as the main intellectual push back in 1977. All were based on the same premise that law was wholly indeterminate, and all legal arrangements therefore were both unjust and ripe for renegotiation. Feminist scholars gave birth to Fem-Crit Studies, homosexuals propounded Critical Queer Theory, and various minority groups each claimed their own branch of the manifold philosophy (for instance, Lat-Crit Theory for Hispanics).

African-American Crits inaugurated Critical Race Theory. This line of thought viewed existing legal structures as tarred with racism, and argued that storytelling narrative in law-review articles reflected the oral traditions of the African-American experience. Because of the lack of meaning in any legal text, these scholars argued, each racial group must figure out for itself the true meaning of the law. Paul Butler, an advocate of Critical Race Theory, wrote one particularly frank analysis of the genre in the *Yale Law Journal* in 1995. A black man and former federal prosecutor, Butler offered a formal defense of racial jury nullification by black jurors who did not wish to see certain black defendants incarcerated. "My thesis is that the black community is better off when some nonviolent law breakers remain in the community rather than go to prison," Butler argued. "The decision as to what kind of conduct by African-Americans ought to be punished is better made by African-Americans themselves, based on the costs and benefits to their community, than by the traditional criminal justice process, which is controlled by white lawmakers and white law enforcers." Butler judged it the "moral responsibility of black jurors to emancipate some guilty black outlaws.... Through jury nullification, I want to dismantle the master's house with the master's tools." One writer noted, in this vein, that the defense strategy of Johnnie Cochran, attorney for O. J. Simpson, was simply "applied critical race theory."

Yet despite these developments, and in a peculiar irony of history, Harvard Law School lost much of its intellectual vigor in the 1960s and 1970s even as it grew in real power in the society around it. In a direct rebuke to the brooding memory of Bull Warren, the admissions office by the 1980s would brag to prospective students in its brochures of its 99 percent graduation rate. Students, once accepted, found it almost impossible not to graduate lest this statistic be imperiled. Thus the "gentleman's B" for the masses was born at Harvard: a default grade virtually guaranteed for students who showed up and took the final examination. The Crits also succeeded in instituting the "no-hassle pass," whereby students who were called on in class but were unprepared could "pass" for the day. All the critiques of traditional legal education leveled by the Crits and their allies—and the "alternative" practices they advocated—inevitably sapped the intellectual regimen of the institution they were attacking.

On the other hand, those students who did strive for top grades or slots on the prestigious *Harvard Law Review* found the competition as strenuous as ever—even more so for those not benefiting from new racial and gender preferences. After passage of the Civil Rights Act of 1964, which prohibited discrimination in employment, much of the civil rights establishment then pressured federal officials and private businesses to hire more minorities irrespective of traditional qualifications. In 1969, the Nixon administration required contractors working on federally assisted projects to set specific goals for minority hiring. This focus on greater numbers rather than equal opportunity seeped into academia, with elite universities and law schools essentially reserving a substantial percentage of their student bodies for minority applicants. While rejecting admission quotas per se, the U.S. Supreme Court upheld quotas de facto in 1978 in *Regents of the University of California v. Bakke.*

Affirmative action eventually crept into the *Harvard Law Review.* Each year, beginning in 1981, applicants for the law review were informed that half of the editor positions would be awarded based on grades, the other half on writing. But if this initial exercise failed to secure a group of new editors with a sufficiently high percentage of women and minorities, the editors would then pick additional women and minorities by considering racial, sexual and "societal" disadvantages the applicants had overcome. Students who wanted these extra factors considered at the outset of the competition could so indicate in a separate statement to the editors of the *Review.* Eight slots out of forty were essentially reserved for minorities as a quota.

Even as its academic standards began to slide, Harvard Law School solidified its status as a legal and cultural power-house. The liberal activism of the federal judiciary, commencing under the leadership of Chief Justice Earl Warren, began an unprecedented expansion of the power of judges and the lawyer class generally. At the same time, Harvard Law professors became round-the-clock fixtures on the nation's television broadcasts. Americans could have breakfast while listening to Arthur Miller, in his familiar three-piece suit, give everyday legal advice on *Good Morning America;* watch Laurence Tribe deliver oral argument before the U.S. Supreme Court on the evening news, on behalf of any number of liberal or Democratic causes; and listen to Alan Dershowitz defend one of his misbehaving celebrity clients or argue one of his provocative views on late-night interview shows. As America became a more legalistic society—as the number of lawsuits filed rose sharply, and as the nation's most important public policy issues were increasingly decided by the judiciary—Harvard Law necessarily became a greater force to be reckoned with.

This growth in influence and notoriety was a profitable arrangement for professors and students. As a result, notwith-standing its inevitable personality conflicts, Harvard Law remained for many years essentially a gentlemen's club, where every professor and student dutifully promoted himself or her-self and, in the process, the school as a whole.

It was not until the late 1980s that this implicit compact would be shattered. The ideological left at Harvard, led by the Crits and their allies in the race and gender study movements, sought to recruit to the school more professors and students who thought as they did. The old establishment consensus of legal realism married to rights-based liberalism—the political "center" at Harvard Law—came under assault from the activists of the left. Those who objected to this expansionism or who otherwise expressed viewpoints deemed right of center found their lives made much more unpleasant at the school. Acrimony arose in both classroom and faculty lounge as the left sought to expand its primacy. In 1984, one professor confided to a journalist that the faculty was engaged in a "struggle for the soul of this institution." Robert Gordon, a professor at Stanford Law School, explained the savagery of the conflict: "There's a peculiar kind of vanity or megalomania at Harvard, that the place is the soul of the American ruling class. Whoever wins the local institutional battles there thinks they will control America's cultural and institutional destiny."

By 2002, self-described conservatives were harder to find on the Harvard faculty than a passenger pigeon. That same year, the British news magazine *The Economist* labeled Harvard Law School no less than "the command centre of American liberalism." In achieving this distinction, the school had changed fundamentally. An institution that formerly celebrated and defended the American traditions of freedom and democracy had become a school uncertain about their value.

There had been clashes before, to be sure. For over twenty years, heated disputes had flared up over the flashpoints of modern society, namely race and gender. These battles usually boiled down to rather pedestrian arguments over whether the law school had hired enough female or minority professors. But as the majority of students and faculty became committed to, and indeed invested in, a vision of America as a nation of victims, a culture developed that was intolerant of dissenting views. Those who challenged race or gender preferences in admissions or hiring, for instance, were in for a good deal of rough treatment, ranging from open hissing to potential discrimination in grading and faculty hiring.

Such intolerance was a radically new regime. In the past, civil discussions and tolerance of great philosophical differences had long been the norm. Indeed, graduates of Harvard Law had become some of the nation's most influential exponents of freedom of speech and democratic institutions. In a 1919 dissent in *Abrams v. United States,* Justice Oliver Wendell Holmes had famously defended the First Amendment as ensuring that America remained a "free market of ideas," where only pragmatic, commonsense principles that worked in practice would gain public favor. Over half a century later, Justice William Brennan, another Harvard graduate, wrote the Supreme Court's opinion in *New York Times v. Sullivan,* which expanded free-speech protections for journalists. Back at their alma mater, however, such vigorous defenses of free speech had given way by the turn of the twenty-first century to a soft totalitarianism in which dissenters were targets of steady harassment.

This new left-wing orthodoxy was pressed so harshly because the stakes were so high. By 2002, the legal and cultural influence that Harvard Law School had acquired in prior decades allowed the school genuinely to mold American society, in ways both obvious and subtle. Law professors there wrote the legal philosophies that became the raw material of future court opinions. Judges pondering a legal issue often consulted the latest ideas and publications in legal academia. Just as trends in fashion and entertainment emanated from Paris and Hollywood, trends in law flowed disproportionately from Harvard.

From behind Harvard's famous colonnaded walls, its law professors sent forth a regular stream of writings urging the courts to rewrite the Constitution and overturn democratically enacted laws. Professor Alan Dershowitz co-authored a seminal article in the *Harvard Law Review* that was cited frequently by the U.S. Supreme Court in *Furman v. Georgia,* the 1972 case in which the Court struck down the death penalty as unconstitutional. (The Court rescinded its ruling four years later.) The Supreme Court has cited the writings of Professor Charles Fried in cases dealing with such diverse topics as savings-and-loan regulations and same-sex intercourse. One Harvard Law professor, Laurence Tribe, has been quoted in sixty-five separate Supreme Court opinions dealing with term limits for congressmen, nude dancing, racial gerrymandering and federalism.

Almost all the influential books and law-review articles authored by Harvard Law professors endorsed a variation of activist liberalism. Court opinions that followed and adopted such reasoning created new rights that remade society in an image more in keeping with the liberal conception of the good life. Based on arguments and reasoning made by Harvard Law professors, courts increasingly were even halting or overturning elections. Professor Tribe personally argued to the U.S. Supreme Court the predecessor case for *Bush v. Gore* following the 2000 presidential election. And in 2003, representing the American Civil Liberties Union, Tribe succeeded temporarily in convincing the U.S. Ninth Circuit Court of Appeals to block the gubernatorial recall election in California.

Harvard Law School also influenced the courts through its steady outpouring of graduates. Law professors at Harvard rarely confined themselves to simply instructing students on the basic principles of law. They often inculcated, consciously or not, a certain worldview and values in their captive audiences. These lessons built on a foundation of liberalism already laid during the students' undergraduate education. By reinforcing and amplifying these views at the law-school level, professors helped ensure that their young charges would promote the same ideas and values in law firms, boardrooms and other notable positions after graduating.

The effect of this pedagogy was especially pronounced among clerks serving the nation's judges. A judicial clerkship is often the first stage of a legal career, especially for a budding law professor or judge. Clerks research and write opinions for judges, who often do little more than edit the opinions before publishing them under their own names. Clerks who are able to insert into court opinions the theories they have learned in law school succeed in making these ideas, instantly, the law of the land.

Harvard sent more of its graduates to clerk for the Supreme Court than any other law school. Predictably, the rulings of the high court often promoted a set of values popular at Harvard but at odds with the views of a majority of Americans. These new legal theories imposed by the high court reflected, in the words of Justice Antonin Scalia (a Harvard Law graduate of an earlier era), "the views and values of the lawyer class from which the Court's Members are drawn."

Harvard Law School was also a powerful cultural symbol in its own right. In addition to the almost ubiquitous presence of its professors on television, the school had inspired or served as the setting of numerous popular books and films. The dean of the school once presented the actor Tom Cruise with a certificate of appreciation for portraying not one but two Harvard Law graduates in different hit movies, *A Few Good Men* and *The Firm*. (In a photograph taken of the event, the actor flashed his enormous trademark smile.) *The Paper Chase* became a hit movie and TV series that at once bolstered Harvard Law's standing as the nation's preeminent law school and deepened the public impression of the school as a center of rigorous instruction and brutal competition. The popular culture looked to Harvard because beneath the larger philosophical battles at the school was the more humdrum, daily strife of ambitious young men and women trying to make their way in the world. The competition over admission, grades and other spoils of this institution provoked ugly ideological struggles, but also was a source of fascination to the public. Lawyers had a disproportionate say in how American society was run, and Harvard lawyers tended to be the ones doing the saying.

KIWI CAMARA'S CLASS NOTES would trigger a chain of events that would illuminate just how hostile to basic civil liberties Harvard Law School had become through its gradual metamorphosis. All the familiar characters who had driven Harvard Law to the far left would come on stage during this period of upheaval. Racial separatists and extremists among students and faculty; neo-Marxist professors promoting Critical Legal Studies; an administration whose philosophy was reminiscent of that of cowed university presidents during the 1960s; traditional liberals silent in response to the mob: all would make an appearance. But there would also be students, faculty and alumni who came to the fore to defend freedom of thought and diversity of viewpoint. This small group would fight back, and would enjoy surprising success.

With one click of his mouse, Camara did more than ruin his own career before it even began. He also set into motion forces that would reveal the extent to which America's oldest law school had become inimical to the core freedoms on which it and the nation had been founded.

CHAPTER ONE

CROCODILE HUNTING

By the spring of 2002, the very look of Harvard Law School suggested a sort of genteel chaos. The school had sprouted some nineteen buildings over the years. These were connected by underground tunnels so that students and faculty could move between them while avoiding the winter chill. Unlike the business school, with its rows of uniform red-brick classrooms and halls, the law school was a hodgepodge of edifices that reflected the changing architectural preferences of the decades in which they were built. The resulting effect was something of a metaphor for American law: an accretion of precedents over the centuries, often displaying no pattern other than the caprice of those in charge at the time.

Even if its classes had been taught in barns, Harvard Law no doubt would have produced a healthy crop of leaders for law and other professions. The school had lured and graduated more future legends of law than any other institution. By 2002, some 22 out of 112 Supreme Court justices had graduated from Harvard. Four of the nine sitting members of the Court were alumni (Antonin Scalia, Anthony Kennedy, David Souter and Stephen Breyer), and another (Ruth Bader Ginsburg) attended Harvard for two years before leaving to join her husband in New York.

Becoming a student or a professor at Harvard Law was a career-making event. Thus it was predictable that the school became an early and prolonged focus of agitation for racial quotas, as minorities sought to increase the odds of being admitted or hired there. The school's affirmative action program was instituted in the late 1960s in response to criticism from civil rights groups and others on the political left over the low number of minority students enrolled at Harvard and other Ivy League schools. But the goal of placating these critics—and the later generations of critics who would voice the same complaints—proved elusive. No matter how many minorities Harvard Law admitted or hired, the school still drew regular complaints from civil rights activists that its affirmative action program was insufficiently generous, and that the institution lacked good will generally toward people of color.

Faculty appointments became an endless source of contention. Many of the men and women admitted to law schools under affirmative action in the 1960s demanded that they be made tenured professors when they subsequently grew in experience and stature within the legal community. Thus did the law school enter the "second stage" of affirmative action. It was now argued that affirmative action in hiring was necessary so that minority professors could serve as "role models" for minority students. The consequent racial friction in hiring and promotions would provide the backdrop for the free speech crisis of 2002.

The first serious row over racial preferences in faculty hiring had occurred two decades before. In the spring of 1983, Dean James Vorenberg hired two men to teach a civil rights course, one of whom was a white liberal: Jack Greenberg, then director counsel for the NAACP Legal Defense Fund. Many African-American students took this appointment as an affront and insisted that a member of their own race be selected for the position. One student wrote to Greenberg urging him not to accept the job because, as a white man, he could not serve as a fitting role model for black students.

Noting that Greenberg had succeeded Thurgood Marshall in his role at the NAACP, Vorenberg stuck by his appointment. Black students upped the ante by boycotting the class. Sit-ins and other protests followed. The law school then tried to make amends by hiring three additional black professors.

Stoking these resentments further was Professor Derrick Bell, who would become the prime mover of racial controversy at Harvard Law and the nemesis of the school's administration. Born in 1930, Bell grew up in a working-class neighborhood in Pittsburgh. He recalled of his family, "They treated me like I was Jesus." As a result, he said, "I always had the feeling that I was fairly special." In 1957, Bell was the only black graduate of the University of Pittsburgh Law School. His classmates wrote of him in the law-school yearbook, "Knows everything and wants others to know he knows everything." He became known for his black-rimmed glasses and somewhat unmanaged hair as well as his self-confidence and taste for confrontation.

Bell's first job was a post in the Civil Rights Division of the Justice Department. But after his superiors asked him to resign his membership in the NAACP due to a potential conflict of interest (the organization was frequently a plaintiff in the many civil rights cases before the federal bar), he refused, and instead left the Justice Department to litigate for the NAACP. While an attorney with the NAACP Legal Defense Fund, Bell became a protégé of Thurgood Marshall.

Following the assassination of Martin Luther King Jr., Harvard's Black Law Students Association urged the school to hire a minority faculty member. Bell had come onto the Harvard radar screen after Professor Charles Nesson, a former civil rights litigator with the Justice Department, invited him to give a guest lecture in his civil rights course. In 1969, the president of Harvard University, Derek Bok, and the president of the Black Law Students Association, Robert Bell (no relation), flew to Los Angeles to offer Derrick Bell a faculty position in person. Two years later, Harvard Law made Bell its first tenured black professor.

Bell acknowledged freely, if somewhat churlishly, that he lacked the qualifications of all previous professors at the school. Unlike other members of the faculty, he had not graduated with distinction from a prestigious law school. Nor had he clerked on the Supreme Court or practiced law at a major firm. Although he mocked these criteria, not having them would make the prickly Bell even more sensitive to imagined slights. His feelings of inferiority would never be far below the surface and would bubble up periodically during his rocky tenure.

In 1980, Bell left Harvard for the University of Oregon School of Law, where he had been named dean—the first black dean of a nonblack law school. Five years later, he resigned amid controversy. While his stated reason for stepping down was the school's failure to grant tenure to an Asian female professor, some professors at Oregon accused him of using this dispute as a convenient excuse to leave by choice before he had to leave by compulsion. Bell, in their judgment, had become an "absentee dean" who spent more time on the lecture circuit than at Oregon.

Bell landed at Stanford Law School in 1986. More unrest followed. Students complained that he was failing to teach actual law in his constitutional law class, that he was disorganized and was dedicating his lectures to indoctrination in his own left-wing theories. The school quietly began to offer a lecture series for his students to supplement his course. An indignant Bell wrote a lengthy essay about the race-related affronts he had suffered at Stanford and dashed it off to every law school in the country. That fall, he switched coasts and returned to Harvard, where he would remain through the end of the decade.

Bell was a loose and unconventional thinker even by the standards of the post-1960s faculty at Harvard. He experimented with student self-grading. He also wrote articles that, by his own admission, were a "style of storytelling" that was "less rigorous than the doctrine-laden, citation-heavy law review pieces" traditionally authored by law professors. His favorite device was conveying legal and social commentary through invented characters who would weave together fact and fiction—with the reader left uncertain where one began and the other ended.

Representative and most renowned of Bell's works in this regard were two allegories published as law-review articles. In "The Final Report: Harvard's Affirmative Action Allegory," Bell related a story in which the president of Harvard convenes a meeting to take up complaints about the school's inadequate affirmative action program. An "earth-shaking explosion" kills the president and all the university's black professors and administrators at the meeting site. Found amid the ruins are documents and tapes preserving the final words and thoughts of the ill-fated assembly: mostly grievances about hiring tokenism and lingering snootiness toward nontraditional scholarship such as storytelling. Further blurring the line between fact and fiction, Bell presented this fable to Harvard's president at the time, Derek Bok. Bell muddied things even more by citing actual statistics of faculty hiring and admission practices in the body of the story *cum* essay.

Bell's masterpiece in this genre was "The Civil Rights Chronicles," published in the *Harvard Law Review* in 1985. Here Bell offered a dialogue between a fictional 1960s-era civil rights lawyer named Geneva Crenshaw and a solicitous, anonymous friend who at times serves as a surrogate for Bell and at other times seems to be Bell himself.

After an automobile accident in Mississippi in 1964 caused by racists intentionally forcing her off the road, Crenshaw suffers for more than twenty years from a form of catatonia that allows her mind to wander "in realms where medical science could not follow." Endowed with such powers, she tells of witnessing an all-black, all-female "Celestial Curia" confronting "Agent H," an emissary of their body who has performed poorly on their behalf on Earth. The Celestial Curia grills Agent H over his failure to promote greater racial justice and compassion for the poor in America. Thus reprimanded, Agent H tries to reassure them by pledging, "I will gain appointment to the land's High Court, and I will wage a ceaseless campaign against the liberal orientation of its decisions." He explains his goal: "By hardening the hearts of the upper classes and by preventing crumbs from falling from their tables, I will awaken the masses to the painful reality of their true status." Agent H serves in this story as an obvious, sinister simulacrum of Chief Justice William Rehnquist.

Crenshaw also bemoans both the resistance to true affirmative action at her university and life as a minority law professor. Clearly functioning as a mouthpiece for Bell and his resentments, Crenshaw accuses her white colleagues on the faculty of jealousy: "For them, nothing I did was right: my articles were flashy but not deep, rhetorical rather than scholarly..... The more successful I appeared, the harsher became the collective judgment of my former friends."

One theme appearing throughout Bell's writings is the accusation that black professors less committed to racial quotas than he are traitors to their race. One of the recurring targets of this ire was fellow African-American Harvard Law professor Randall Kennedy, who had emerged as a voice of moderation during the recent spate of protests at the school, or at least as somebody unwilling to participate in them. In an article in the *Harvard Law Review* published in 1989, Kennedy noted Bell's tendency to offer "mere assertion" in defense of his claim that "traditional standards" for faculty appointments are biased. Kennedy observed that it is "self-defeating" to "leave unexplored why it is that criteria that seem innocuous and relevant on their face have such disastrous consequences for minority candidates." When Bell later spoke of professors who "look black but think white," it was widely assumed by fellow professors such as Alan Dershowitz that he was directing these words at Kennedy.

Bell's scholarship and activism at Harvard reflected his ambivalent view of America. He spoke of white Americans as people protective of their collective interests. In his book *Faces at the Bottom of the Well: The Permanence of Racism,* he branded whites "members of the oppressor class." African-Americans who disapproved of affirmative action were, in his mind, quislings to their race. After Clarence Thomas was appointed to the Supreme Court in 1991, Bell denounced him as being, among other things, unqualified. He claimed,

> Given Thomas's modest academic background, relative youth, lack of litigation experience, and undistinguished service in appointive government positions, only his "enhanced standing" ... as a well-known critic of affirmative action and civil rights policies and leaders in general could have won him priority over the multitude of lawyers, white and black, with more traditional qualifications for a seat on our highest Court.

And yet, except for the reference to Thomas's opposition to racial preferences, an identical (and much more accurate) assessment could have been made of the underqualified Bell after his appointment to the Harvard faculty.

As he prosecuted his guerrilla war against what he saw as an oppressive status quo, Bell became convinced that Harvard Law was unfair to minorities seeking professorships there. He made the school's failure to hire a "woman of color" for the faculty into a symbolic issue. In 1990, when he began his crusade, women constituted 45 percent of the Harvard Law School student body and minorities 22 percent. But he ignored these remarkably positive figures and focused on the ratios on the faculty, where there was less turnover than in the student body and therefore fewer opportunities to engineer his vision of diversity. He rested his case against the law school on the fact that only 4 black men and 5 women had been given tenured positions on a faculty of 57.

The cause of this discrimination, Bell believed, was the use of "traditional qualifications" such as outstanding grades and test scores, selection for law reviews and Supreme Court clerkships in evaluating potential professors. He contended that standardized tests were "stacked against women and people of color." Moreover, "Biases inhere in every aspect of the qualification process, from college (and thus law school) admission, to course grades." Some of the main beneficiaries of these hopelessly biased policies were the "substantial number of Jewish professors" on the Harvard Law faculty. Bell offered this commentary, it bears noting, at a time when tensions between blacks and Jews were rising nationally—amid the background noise of Jesse Jackson's reference to New York City as "Hymietown," Louis Farrakhan's emergence as a popular spokesman for black causes, and the anti-Semitic violence of Crown Heights.

Bell decried the "clear class connection between high grades earned at a prestigious law school and the equally clear exclusionary effect of the traditional standards on both minorities and whites who have the potential for excellent teaching and scholarship." He argued that nontraditional standards should be tailored to ensure a proportionate representation of minorities at these schools—in other words, that the only standards that mattered were those that achieved racial balance. He added that "the almost hysterical opposition to faculty diversity is impressive proof of its need." Such was the circular reasoning that Bell employed: Anybody who dared disagree with him and his extreme advocacy of racial quotas was a racist who simply bolstered his case for change.

The final provocation for Bell was what he regarded as Harvard's mistreatment of the black law professor Regina Austin. An honors graduate of the University of Pennsylvania Law School, Austin was subsequently invited to teach at Harvard as a visiting professor from 1989 to 1990 as part of the school's diversity campaign. In an effort to get Harvard Law to hire a permanent "woman of color," Bell worked to strong-arm the law school to waive its rules for faculty selections and offer Austin a permanent position. Despite a longstanding policy that forbade Harvard from hiring visiting professors during the year of their residence at the school, Bell insisted that Austin be hired permanently. This was, in the language of the 1960s he sometimes employed, a "nonnegotiable demand."

Even had the rules been different, Austin still would likely not have earned a place on the faculty. Harvard's appointments committee was not impressed with her tenure piece, an article in the *Stanford Law Review* that laid out a claim for intentional infliction of emotional distress caused by racial discrimination and sexual abuse. In the end, the school refused to grant her a permanent position.

Bell promptly announced in April 1990 that he had seen enough and that he would leave Harvard unless major changes were made to ensure greater diversity in the faculty. The announcement made national news, earning space on the front page of the *New York Times*. Jesse Jackson flew in and offered to negotiate Bell's differences with the administration. The new dean, Robert Clark, met with Jackson before a press conference and rally but declined to negotiate with Bell through him.

By the time Bell took leave of Harvard, he had become, as the ensuing publicity attested, a national cause célèbre on the left. He clearly delighted in this role, as well as in building up legions of loyal supporters who would continue to cause trouble for the Harvard Law administration in his absence.

During the following academic year, Bell's admirers in the student body kept the heat on. They organized a Coalition for Civil Rights, held rallies and silent vigils outside faculty meetings, and conducted overnight sit-ins at the dean's office. A group of students sued the law school and the university. They claimed hiring discrimination, alleging that by excluding a disproportionate percentage of qualified women and minorities for tenure and tenure-track positions, Harvard had violated state civil rights laws. The suit was dismissed, but the students had made their point, generating more news and more pressure.

Through the 1990–91 school year, Bell taught a civil rights course at the school without pay. But his well-publicized gesture of giving up his $120,000 annual salary during this year-long "leave of absence" was undermined when he later acknowledged that a "major entertainment figure" had put him on his payroll for "consulting" services. These "services," Bell conceded, amounted to giving advice that was ignored.

In fact, Bell would not have been satisfied even with the hiring of Regina Austin. A law-review article he authored several years later lambasted law schools that hired only "token" minorities, as Austin clearly was by her own self-description (she referred to herself forlornly as a "token token," being both black and female). "The hiring of a few minorities and women—particularly when a faculty is under pressure from students or civil rights agencies—is not a departure from, but an adherence to, this power-preserving doctrine" of de facto white male supremacy, Bell wrote. In other words, law schools that relented to the demands of Bell and company and hired personnel such as Austin were *still* in the thrall of bigotry. This presented truly a no-win situation for Harvard Law, unless perhaps the school began laying off large numbers of white professors.

In the spring of 1991, Bell decided to make a geographical break to drive his point home. He announced that he would teach for a year at the New York University Law School. This year became two. Then Bell requested leave to teach for a third year at NYU. He now was asking not only for waiver of the visiting-professor tenure rule, but also for waiver of the firm rule forbidding more than two years for a professor to be on leave. (Henry Kissinger's request for an extension from the university was turned down while he was serving as U.S. secretary of state, and Charles Fried was constrained to resign his professorship at the law school while he served as solicitor general under President Ronald Reagan.)

Bell commanded considerable support from the very faculty whose lack of diversity he was assailing. With Randall Kennedy's courageous exception, the other black professors at Harvard Law sided with Bell. This included a new faculty member named Charles Ogletree, who had been hired as an assistant professor in 1989 and did not have tenure. The proponents of Critical Legal Studies also stood in solidarity with their fellow troublemaker of the left. Even the soft-spoken leftist Professor Frank Michelman tried to negotiate the differences between Bell and the administration to keep the dyspeptic Bell happy. But more and more, it appeared that Bell was asking to become a law unto himself.

On March 11, 1991, the ubiquitous Jesse Jackson returned to Harvard Law School to stump once again for the beleaguered Derrick Bell. Wearing a navy blue wool suit, Jackson stood before a crowd of nearly 450 students in the Ames Courtroom in Austin Hall and urged the audience to oppose "apartheid in the Law School faculty." Then he broke into one of his patented cadences, saying, "Harvard is too high on the hill to cast shades of darkness when we need points of light."

The dean of the law school, Robert Clark, would not waive the two-year leave policy. Clark informed Bell that if he did not return to Harvard, he would be terminated. When Bell did not comply, he was informed that his position on the faculty had been lost.

Bell's revenge was the intellectual minefield he had sowed back at Harvard. His one-man insurrection had left the law school a racially balkanized and politically hypersensitive institution. Bell became an important symbol of intractable racial resentment at America's campuses. The bitter clash he had touched off, moreover, marked an important chapter in the nation's long-running conflict over race. Harvard Law School was now, more than ever, one of the chief fronts in the culture war.

Bell left behind a school that had never been more polarized. The left hailed him for his stewardship of its cause, while a writer for the *Wall Street Journal* characterized his actions and the related controversy as a "vile circus." By 2002, Bell had settled in at his lesser perch outside Cambridge, but the sparks left from his fiery trajectory through Harvard still flickered. The law school had not fully recovered from these fights when Kiwi Camara e-mailed his notes to HLCentral.

AFTER MICHELLE SIMPSON finished reading Kiwi Camara's notes, her indignation hardened into resolve. Not content simply to complain to the school's webmaster about "nigs," she sent an e-mail to the other members of her section, alerting them to Camara's offense and complaining about his insensitivity. Camara and Simpson were in the same 1L section, a group of about eighty students who took their standard first-year courses together: Contracts, Civil Procedure, Criminal Law, Torts, Property, and Moot Court. By informing Camara's section mates of his actions, Simpson ensured that his social life, not to mention his professional opportunities, would never be the same.

Simpson then broadened her offensive. Seeking formal action from the law school, she filed a complaint with the administration.

As news of Simpson's complaint spread among the student body, Camara received unexpected and unwelcome support from another student in their section that guaranteed that his contretemps would ignite a schoolwide controversy. On April 1, Simpson and other members of Section IV got an anonymous e-mail that discussed the Camara notes. It bore only a few clues of authorship. The e-mail referred to life at Harvard, suggesting that the writer was a student there. And the author had an unusual online name: "gcrocodile."

"I am deeply saddened that as a result of your complaint Kiwi Camara has decided not to share his outlines with the HLS community in the future," gcrocodile declared. "Shame on you! You have done a great disservice both to HLS and to the African-American community."

The statement continued: "If you, as a race, want to prove that you do not deserve to be called by that word, work hard and you will be recognized. If you just complain and ask others to do the job for you, it will have the opposite effect."

The author then emptied gasoline on Camara's kindling: "We are at the Harvard Law School, a free, private community where any member wishing to use the word 'nigger' in any form should not be prevented from doing so. To give you an example, as a result of your complaint I have actually begun using the 'nigger' word more often than before the incident."

Another black 1L, Olufunke Grace Bankole, had posted a request that unsolicited e-mails not be sent to her Harvard e-mail account. When she nevertheless received a copy of gcrocodile's e-mail, she replied to the anonymous sender asking that she not be sent further e-mails in the future. Gcrocodile answered, "bite me."

An insular academic community that regarded inadequate support for affirmative action as proof of racism was now confronting the real thing, or something very close to it. This message, apparently authored by a Harvard Law student, had been transmitted freely on the school's Internet service. Phones rang and e-mails zipped as the offended African-American students of Harvard Law commiserated with one another and planned a response.

On the morning of April 2, mere hours after gcrocodile transmitted his e-mail, students in Section IV found that anonymous flyers had been clandestinely distributed in their mailboxes. The students often began their day by clustering in front of these mailboxes, which were located in Harkness Commons, an unpretentious rectangular building that housed a small convenience store, a bookstore and a student commons area. This morning, the students found that their mailboxes had become a cache of anti-Semitism.

The flyers, printed on plain white paper, prominently featured the text of gcrocodile's e-mail. Alongside it was a miscellany of profanities and anti-Semitic statements and insignia. Written in large letters were the words, "Fuck Jews." Next to these words was a swastika. Below was the message, "I hope you rot in hell with your yamukas [*sic*]. I bet that you will respond to this leaflet because Jews, unlike blacks, are a politically and economically favored group at this university."

As a tactic designed to draw greater attention to the gcrocodile e-mail, the flyers succeeded tremendously. No longer was this a matter of a few Section IV students exchanging harsh words via e-mail, or a handful of disgruntled minority students enraged that their complaints were ignored. Harvard Law School was now aflame with recriminations and angry calls for revenge that would spread far beyond Kiwi Camara and Michelle Simpson, eventually affecting the lives and careers of many others in the Harvard Law community.

CHAPTER TWO

UP IN SMOKE

Professor Charles Nesson—brilliant, amiable, unconventional, liberal—was a representative figure for Harvard Law. In the spring of 2002, he could not have foreseen being sucked into the emerging racial maelstrom. Yet this outcome was all but unavoidable. The man couldn't help himself.

Nesson had climbed the traditional rungs to a tenured professorship at Harvard. Through all three years at the law school, he earned the top grades in his class. After graduating in 1963, he clerked on the U.S. Supreme Court for Justice John Marshall Harlan. A stint in government followed, as Nesson departed for Alabama to serve as a special assistant in the Civil Rights Division of the Justice Department. The first case he worked on, *White v. Crook,* became a watershed civil rights triumph, in which Alabama's race- and gender-based methods for picking juries were struck down as unconstitutional. He joined the Harvard Law School faculty in 1966.

Nesson's subsequent litigation showed the same commitment to liberal principles. When Daniel Ellsberg, the Pentagon analyst turned flamboyant antiwar activist who surreptitiously released the Pentagon Papers to the press in 1971, was indicted for espionage and theft, he asked Nesson to serve as both attorney and advisor. Nesson later recalled counseling Ellsberg on "all the ins and outs ... of what it would mean if he went underground," on how to dodge the FBI as he covertly leaked the top-secret material to various newspapers beginning with the *New York Times*. Ellsberg settled in a friend's apartment not far from Harvard Law School. To help him avoid detection by authorities, Nesson and another attorney assisting Ellsberg would walk their bicycles through the underground tunnels connecting the buildings at the law school, "come up, and then ride them the wrong way down one-way streets and in pathways through buildings til we were convinced that nobody could possibly be connected with us. And then we'd go to Dan's apartment. We'd sit and meet with him."

Nesson enjoyed the cloak-and-dagger maneuvering. On a later occasion, he phoned an Ellsberg sympathizer and established contact for his client by reading a poem the other man would recognize, "Trip City"—code for the Pentagon Papers. In his biography of Ellsberg, *Wild Man,* Tom Wells portrayed Nesson as adventuresome and loyal to Ellsberg. But Ellsberg's ex-wife, Carol, remembered Nesson as unctuous and "a little on the slick side," someone who at times misled her about whether she or her children would have to testify in Ellsberg's trial. This uncharitable depiction is understandable in light of the fact that Nesson served as something of a facilitator of Ellsberg's extramarital dalliances, while working nonetheless to procure Carol's helpful testimony. Nesson was somewhat less accomplished in the courtroom. The federal judge hearing the Ellsberg case, W. Matthew Byrne, often had to assist him in properly framing the questions he put to witnesses. (The judge eventually dismissed the case against Ellsberg.)

Nesson later collaborated with plaintiff's attorney Jan Schlichtmann in one of the most celebrated environmental tort cases in U.S. history, further bolstering his credentials as an all-star litigator of the left. The case, arising from seepage of industrial chemicals into the water supply of Woburn, Massachusetts, would inspire a famous book and a movie of the same name, *A Civil Action*. Though Nesson and Schlichtmann both worked in Boston, Schlichtmann flew to a legal seminar in San Juan, Puerto Rico, to improve his prospects of effectively buttonholing Nesson and persuading him to join the case. "Billion-dollar Charlie" was the moniker that Nesson earned from Schlichtmann's co-counsel after arguing in a strategy meeting that the potential punitive damages against the two defendant corporations were where the money really was—a total that, in Nesson's estimation, approached half a billion dollars.

This aspiration and a general hostility toward corporate America colored Nesson's approach inside the courtroom, and contributed mightily to the plaintiffs' missteps in the Woburn case. The judge, Walter Jay Skinner, was an alumnus of Harvard Law and familiar with one of Nesson's seminal writings on tort law through his subscription to the *Harvard Law Review*. He was originally predisposed in Nesson's favor, but things degenerated quickly after Nesson first rose to offer oral argument on a number of motions in the case. "I consider it my job to get this verdict with no error that can possibly upset it on appeal," Nesson offered presumptuously in his opening speech to the court. ("If you can prevent me from making an error, that's fine," the judge replied good-naturedly.)

Weeks later, as Nesson continued his harangue against ne'er-do-well corporations, Skinner scolded him sharply. "I take umbrage at the entire tone of your presentation," he told Nesson with evident irritation. "You were trumpeting away about sending messages to the boardrooms of America.

Lawsuits are between parties, Professor.... If the boardrooms of America happen to notice what's going on, that's an incidental consequence of the process. It's not the purpose of it." Not only did Nesson poison relations with the trial judge, but Schlichtmann and the other plaintiffs' attorneys miscalculated the strength and value of their case due largely to his misreading of the facts. After their claims against one of the corporations were dismissed entirely, they found themselves downsizing their expectations—those billion-dollar sugarplums still dancing in their heads at Nesson's suggestion.

Still, such grand dreams were what made Nesson a lawyer of national proportions. A striver whose achievements in law reflected tremendous drive, he once penned and distributed to his students, on the last day of a criminal law class, a poem he had written. It was a telling ode to ambition:

> Reach for what you want.
> Want more than you can get.
> Reach, and learn what you can ...
> What do you want?
> More than you can get.
> But then how?
> Take it in pieces,
> Want it all.

Ironically, given what he was about to face, Nesson had arguably acquired more solid bona fides on the subject of civil rights than any other white professor at Harvard Law School. In addition to fighting segregation on behalf of the Justice Department, he had personally lobbied for broad affirmative action at the school, and had actively recruited black professors in the 1960s. It was Nesson, of course, who had invited Derrick

Bell to give his first guest lecture at Harvard Law in Nesson's own civil rights course. He had supported Bell during his stand-off with the Harvard Law administration years later.

Disregard for hierarchy and tradition were also part of Nesson's persona, along with an avant-garde teaching style and quirky notions of interfaculty relations. In one memorable stunt in 2001, Nesson entered his classroom late and began handing out his students' papers in random order, instructing the students to read and grade each other's papers, then rank them. When one student asked whether these rankings would influence their final grades, Nesson replied that he was not sure. Then he left the classroom.

Pandemonium ensued. One student stood and denounced "tyrannical professors." Another was more sympathetic to the enterprise, saying he judged this a "legitimate experiment." Another was more blasé, viewing the episode simply as "a way for Charlie to not grade papers."

Nesson was no less vexatious to his fellow professors. In September 2001, Jesse Jackson, at the invitation of Professor Charles Ogletree, was scheduled to speak at the law school during a time when classes were also scheduled. Professor Elizabeth Warren sent an e-mail to Ogletree asking if the event could be rescheduled to prevent a conflict with her class time. This provoked a flurry of e-mails between the two over the timing of Jackson's appearance.

Nesson, who received copies of the e-mails, decided to share them with his students. The furious Warren demanded a meeting with Nesson. When the two met to discuss the ethics of divulging the e-mails, Nesson secretly tape-recorded their conversation. He then put both the recording of their conversation and the original e-mails on his Web site and encouraged students and faculty members to visit it.

More notorious still was Nesson's admission of ongoing illegal drug use while he was a professor at Harvard. Earlier in his teaching career, Nesson had denied using drugs—even after the annual student parody openly joked about his well-known doping. In 2002, he finally confessed the details of his drug use to the Harvard student newspaper, describing regular morning strolls through Mount Auburn Cemetery, where he smoked marijuana before traipsing off to class. He also acknowledged experimenting with numerous other drugs, including LSD and cocaine. Nesson's confession that he enjoyed taking "a puff or two of a joint" on a more or less daily basis earned a rebuke from Dean Robert Clark: "I strongly believe it is inappropriate for a member of Harvard's Faculty of Law to use a controlled substance in violation of the law under any circumstances," Clark wrote.

For all his flamboyant ways, Nesson was a traditional liberal. During the faculty wars of the 1980s, he took exception to some of the Crits' behavior, urging them to be "more open and generous to others, personally and intellectually," and less responsible for a faculty culture of "vilification, name-calling, back-stabbing, and character assassination." Nesson told his evidence class in 1987 that as a result of these faculty squabbles, he "dropped out of Harvard Law School." He mused, "I was alive somewhere else"—apparently meaning that he had tried to mentally check out of the embattled institution but for his teaching duties there.

By 2002, this sixty-three-year-old flower child had accumulated plenty of gray in his shaggy brown hair and telltale bags under his mischievous eyes. But he could point to decades of solid work at the law school, as well as minor national renown for serving as the facilitator in a series of debates over ethical issues on the Public Broadcasting System. When the

Camara/gcrocodile controversy arose, Nesson saw himself as a natural mediator.

This miscalculation reflected a broader problem with Nesson's judgment and caused some to wonder if it was clouded by drugs. One of his fellow professors privately acknowledged the obvious: "Nesson was going a little crazy that year."

As the racial controversy began to spread beyond Kiwi Camara and Michelle Simpson, Nesson, who was teaching torts to the students of Section IV, decided to use his class as a podium to defuse the situation. In class, he appealed to the author of the anonymous "gcrocodile" e-mail to come forward and speak to him about the matter privately.

Matthias Scholl, who soon would be unveiled as the writer, was a most unlikely provocateur. A Polish immigrant in his forties, Scholl seemed as colorless and inoffensive as anyone who had ever filled a seat in a Harvard classroom. He spent little time at the law school beyond what was required for his coursework. He worked part-time at a major law firm in Boston, specializing in patent and copyright law. That this quiet loner had fired off such vicious e-mails was hard to believe. But Simpson and her allies, armed with solid evidence, prepared to demand official action.

And now, Nesson was implicated as well. In response to his plea, Scholl had decided to reveal his identity voluntarily. On April 4, 2002, Nesson walked into the classroom of another professor, Bernard Harcourt, who taught criminal law to Section IV and proceeded to hijack Harcourt's class, a move as unorthodox as anything he had ever done.

"I've met with gcrocodile," Nesson informed the students. "Now he'd like to say a few words." Nesson asked that the author be given five minutes to explain himself.

Scholl rose. On the advice of Nesson, he kept his comments short. Through his Polish accent, he attempted to explain his actions, insisting that he had not meant to offend anyone. He assured the class that he was not prejudiced, and, in an apparently sincere but ill-advised aside, added that his officemate was black.

Then Nesson took the floor again. He proposed that the class hold a mock trial over the incident. There could be a prosecutor to press the case against Scholl. Nesson himself volunteered to serve as Scholl's defense counsel.

Nesson believed that Scholl's statements, though outrageous and repugnant, were nonetheless protected by the First Amendment. This posture was consistent with Nesson's broad defense of liberty throughout his legal career. In this instance, however, he had made a fateful error. It was one thing to defend someone who had released classified material; it was another thing altogether to defend a politically incorrect person in a highly charged academic environment such as Harvard Law School.

Simpson and other black students in the class reacted immediately and harshly to Nesson's proposal. One of Simpson's friends burst into tears and ran from the classroom. Simpson raised her hand and, she later recalled, became "very emotional." She flatly refused to accept Scholl's apology, telling her classmates, "If you're going to say something hateful and going to apologize for it later, then just don't say it at all." She remained in the classroom fuming, and planning her next move.

With a classmate, Simpson decided to seek support from the faculty and administration. They met with several professors as well as with Todd Rakoff, dean of the J.D. program, and Suzanne Richardson, dean of students. They bitterly protested the racial incidents of that spring and Nesson's proposed mock trial. Professor Harcourt, not amused by the spectacle that Nesson had caused in his class, seconded the students in arguing that the mock trial should not take place. "This is not a pedagogic moment," he said of the controversy that had led to Nesson's proposal.

Scholl spoke publicly about the gcrocodile e-mails only once after the incident. In an interview for the law school newspaper, the *Record*, he expressed regret, blaming his imperfect English for his poor choice of words. He reiterated that his personal relationships insulated him from charges of bigotry. "I'm not a racist," he declared. "My wife is Asian, my best friend is from India and I share an office with an African-American whose friendship, knowledge and resources I value."

As for the "bite me" e-mail to a second black student, Scholl admitted that this was "embarrassing," adding somewhat lamely, "Had I known she was African-American and there would be some sort of racial controversy, I would not have sent either of the e-mails."

Scholl mostly remained unrepentant, however. He regretted that his e-mails had caused him trouble, but did not seem to regret much else. He steadfastly defended his right to use such language, saying of the word "nigger": "I would use the word to show people I have a right to use it, but I don't condone it."

For his part, Nesson would later explain his error in judgment thus: "I acted with good intention but without due care." Such a mea culpa was not acceptable to the mob that would soon demand Nesson's professional head. Nesson seemed oblivious to the fact that the old notions of due process and freedom of speech that defined the liberalism of his generation had mutated into a leftism far more harsh and unforgiving of politically incorrect dissent. What he had not counted on—perhaps had not realized, given that his own views had never before clashed with the prevailing orthodoxy at the law school—was that as liberalism had evolved at Harvard and elsewhere, the rules inside the ivy-covered walls had become different from elsewhere in America. At Harvard, there was less freedom.

CHAPTER THREE

THE LIMITS
OF TENURE

As the students of Section IV fomented and reacted to this crisis, the 1Ls of Section II soon found themselves also swept up in the broadening storm. On March 13, 2002, two weeks before Nesson barged into Bernard Harcourt's classroom, Professor David Rosenberg touched off a second fiery debate by running afoul of other unstated canons of discourse at Harvard Law. This time, the offender was not a smiling *bon vivant* of the 1960s but a crotchety stickler for rigor and principle in a school where respect for both was fading.

David Rosenberg was a sixty-year-old professor who did not suffer fools well, if at all. A solitary figure, Rosenberg kept to himself and preferred that students and professors honor these bounds. He was a hardheaded proponent of the old ways of teaching and dismayed by the efforts to redefine academic excellence that were being advanced by Derrick Bell and company. Though a traditional liberal of the kind that had always found Harvard Law a comfortable habitat, Rosenberg was a staunch believer in the absolute principles of intellectual integrity that, he believed, a successful life in law demanded.

The unyielding quality of his personality made him controversial among students who increasingly were addicted to the sunny laissez-faire that dominated the classroom of Nesson and others. "He delights in pissing students off," was one student's observation of Rosenberg's pedagogy. He was known for scribbling frank and often rude comments in the margins of student papers; and his pupils braced themselves for his marginalia when their work was returned. Exclamations such as "This is crap" were crude attempts to challenge his students to evaluate their positions more clearly. Aspersions such as "commie" and "pinko" sometimes popped up as a way of challenging leftist students to think through their convictions. Yet as one of his students put it, this passion showed that "he cares about the law." Rosenberg was, in short, an abrasive scholar whose impatience with cant could be wounding but who nonetheless was universally respected for possessing one of the finest minds on the faculty.

Though largely aloof from other faculty members, Rosenberg was devoted to seeing his pupils succeed. "He's completely disgusted with university and faculty politics, and pays attention to his teaching and his students," Harvey Silverglate noted of his friend. An alumnus of Harvard Law, Silverglate had represented numerous students in disputes with the Harvard University administration over violations of their free-speech rights, and helped establish the Foundation for Individual Rights in Education to litigate such claims across the country. For all his irascibility, Silverglate observed, Rosenberg was easily accessible to serious students seeking academic or career guidance. Silverglate also praised him for being one of the very few members of the Harvard Law faculty willing to assist him in cases in which Harvard's administrative board charged students with wrongdoing in speech-related matters. "There were few faculty members I could always count on and students could always count on," Silverglate recalled. "And he was one of them."

As an extension of his own philosophy, and perhaps partly out of sheer orneriness, Rosenberg vigorously defended academic freedom and resented recent encroachments on these liberties by the campus left. Over the years, he had frequently locked horns with left-wing extremists of the school. In the 1990s, when the law school instituted sexual harassment policies, for instance, he was one of only a handful of law professors who opposed them on civil liberties grounds, going so far as to boycott the faculty meeting in which the policies were approved.

Spurning lazy theorizing, Rosenberg called for more concrete, real-world analysis of the costs and benefits of court rulings and legislation. He sympathized with the movement called "law and economics," which examined the everyday cost of legal rules in economic rather than normative terms. In one of his most influential articles, he argued for class-action suits because they allowed for a greater collectivization of plaintiffs, and a more efficient and just handling of mass-exposure tort cases, than individual lawsuits. A critic of "junk science," or expert testimony admitted in court in support of questionable but profitable theories of liability, Rosenberg decried by way of example "the spectacle of silicone breast implant plaintiffs asserting claims that were scientifically dubious but that nevertheless resulted in a multi-billion dollar settlement (while bankrupting a major pharmaceutical company)." This outcome, he contended, "raises questions about the wisdom of allowing tort law to venture into areas of scientific debate and impose its traditional all-or-nothing judgments regardless of the degree of scientific uncertainty."

A disciple of Oliver Wendell Holmes, Rosenberg believed that tort classes should "concentrate on the systematic risks from business activity" and "the theories and policies of market regulation." He lamented the fact that instead, "students spend most of their time today parsing the semantic logic of cases to derive, classify, and criticize rules."

More particularly, Rosenberg was one of the few liberal professors who had spoken up in opposition to Critical Legal Studies. He was also a leading force in resisting the granting of tenure to underqualified Crit professors. Rosenberg had played a role in defeating the bid of one prominent Crit applicant, Clare Dalton, who quickly became a martyr to the movement. In 1987, Dalton, an assistant professor at Harvard Law and wife of Robert Reich (subsequent U.S. labor secretary in the Clinton administration), was up for tenure. Traditionalists on the faculty judged Dalton's work unimpressive and below Harvard's standards. Rosenberg went through a painstaking analysis of Dalton's work, producing an eighty-nine-page memorandum questioning her scholarship. Dalton lost the tenure vote by four. Howls of protest rang out from the Crits and leftists at Harvard and sympathizers at other schools. Derrick Bell, for his part, held a four-day sit-in to express his "disappointment and shame" at what had happened, calling the action a "threat to ideological diversity."

Rosenberg, who had devoted his life to studying law, took strong exception to the Crits' reductionist view of the object of his labors. The law had flaws, to be sure, but could not be dismissed as thoroughly illegitimate. He and others faulted Critical Legal Studies for offering nothing to take the place of the legal structure that they proposed to tear down, other than a vague, self-serving Marxism that was no improvement over the existing order.

Harvey Silverglate, who practiced law with Rosenberg in the 1960s, recalled that in 2002, Rosenberg remained an old-fashioned liberal who had not bent with the changing ideological winds. "He has not changed substantially since I first met him," Silverglate observed. "The world has changed." Though Rosenberg "adheres to the principles that he and I believed and practiced in the sixties" (both were and remained ardent supporters of civil rights and civil liberties), the definition of liberalism had changed in subsequent decades. Silverglate said of Rosenberg:

> There is a lot of postmodern nonsense that has crept into the left that he rejects. He rejects the speech codes; he rejects the political correctness; he rejects the cowardice, the fear of doing the right thing, the fear of offending some group. He's the same person he was, remarkably the same person.

But the world of Harvard Law was not the same world it had been back in the sixties. Having refused to "tailor his conscience" to fit the times, Rosenberg found himself whipsawed by the shift in political fashions.

For his support of traditional standards and academic freedom, as well as his opposition to the Crits, Rosenberg came to be regarded at Harvard as a conservative. In a law school in which virtually the entire faculty, including Rosenberg, was liberal on most issues, this designation was true only in a relative sense—one unique to such an isolated academic environment. But this commonly held view of Rosenberg would prove damaging to him as events unfolded in the coming months.

On March 13, 2002, as Michelle Simpson was beginning her chain of complaints about Kiwi Camara's notes in Section IV, Rosenberg led his Section II torts class in a discussion of legal philosophy. The focus of his lecture was John Rawls' classic book *A Theory of Justice,* which laid the intellectual foundations for the Great Society and much of modern liberalism.

As the class discussion meandered, one student spoke up in defense of Critical Legal Studies and asked why Rosenberg was ignoring the movement's contributions to law.

Predictably, Rosenberg defended himself forcefully and without much regard for student sensitivities. "Feminists haven't put forth any positive theory of law," he replied, "they just tear down other people's theories. Marxists put forth nothing, either. Feminists, Marxists and the blacks have contributed nothing to torts."

After a tense silence had settled over the class, a black student, Tel Cary-Sadler, raised his hand. He asked for some clarification. "Mr. Rosenberg, what you said could be taken in an offensive way," he said.

"Good," Rosenberg replied.

Cary-Sadler again asked for clarification of Rosenberg's remarks. "Would you like to restate it?" he asked.

To a proud iconoclast like Rosenberg, such questions, however well motivated and politely stated, only further drew his ire. He repeated the same statement he had made, distinctly and word for word: "Feminists, Marxists and the blacks have contributed nothing to torts."

Again, an edgy quiet gripped the classroom for several seconds as the students absorbed the exchange. One student who thought highly of Rosenberg, Nels Peterson, nevertheless saw the perils of his blunt comments. "The way that he said it, it was pretty clear there was potential for misunderstanding," he recalled.

There would be no backing down for either professor or student. Offending students was an integral part of Rosenberg's teaching methods. He was adamant that the comments themselves, while rough, were not racist. The confrontation in the classroom that day would end in a standoff. But the conflict would soon spill over into the school's administrative offices.

After class, Cary-Sadler and other students upset with Rosenberg's remarks went to the dean of the J.D. program, Todd Rakoff. He was sympathetic and assured them that appropriate action would be taken.

The following day in Rosenberg's class, Cary-Sadler asked for permission to read a statement to the class. Rosenberg consented. Cary-Sadler again took issue with Rosenberg's choice of words. His dander having subsided a bit, Rosenberg this time responded more evenly, saying that he had been criticizing Critical Legal Studies theorists who were black, not an entire race. His explanation, like Nesson's, failed to mollify the forces that now smelled blood.

By the end of March 2002, in two separate sections of first-year students, two highly regarded professors of torts would be accused, essentially, of committing torts of their own. Given that so many graduates of Harvard Law School, like so many lawyers of all backgrounds, had enriched themselves through personal-injury litigation, perhaps there was some cosmic significance to these parallel developments. Nesson recalled that he had "proposed to make the alleged tort into something we use to learn about torts and learn about ourselves"—an exercise that backfired horrendously.

CHAPTER FOUR

BONELESS BOB

For years, the Black Law Students Association (BLSA) had been the most powerful student organization at Harvard Law School. Founded in 1967 by ten black students seeking, in the words of one, a "comfort zone," BLSA quickly grew into a substantial political force at the institution. The group's first political initiative was complaining to Dean Derek Bok about the absence of black workers on a law-school construction site. This was followed up with requests that the school close after the assassination of Martin Luther King Jr. Other members protested the Vietnam War. In the late 1980s and early 1990s, BLSA became the main student agency behind Derrick Bell, engaging in protests and coordinating operations with him and other left-wing elements of the school.

By 2002, BLSA had grown into a formidable interest group that no one with any sense wished to antagonize. In simple terms, no dean or professor could be painted with charges of racism and expect to survive professionally. Moreover, such an allegation, if it stuck, was more than a death sentence for the professor in question. If the administration were widely seen as insensitive to the concerns of minorities, the reputation of the whole institution could be tarnished.

For all these reasons, African-American students and faculty collectively enjoyed a unique status at the school. When they organized and made demands, the administration never failed to take notice. While Derrick Bell had brandished this power with unprecedented efficacy, the students who succeeded him would outdo him in essential respects.

When BLSA stepped into the Camara controversy, it guaranteed that the matter would become Harvard Law's equivalent of an international incident. In an open letter to Dean Robert Clark dated April 11, 2002, BLSA listed nine formal demands of the administration. They were bold and sweeping, and would largely set the law school's agenda for the coming year.

The BLSA letter began by recapitulating the offensive incidents of the preceding two months revolving around Kiwi Camara, Matthias Scholl, Charles Nesson and David Rosenberg. The students also brought up another incident. In March, at the HLS Legal Aid Bureau, a student-run operation providing free legal counsel to indigent clients, one Harvard Law student mistook a black 1L for a potential client. Even though the student who erred apologized both to the 1L and to BLSA, the association cited this mistake as additional proof of a racially hostile climate at the law school. BLSA noted further that the Legal Aid Bureau had "failed to institute any significant internal changes" to prevent such incidents in the future.

Broad reforms were necessary, BLSA claimed, if the school was serious about combating such "pervasive" prejudice. BLSA demanded that the administration begin by officially censuring Camara, Scholl, Nesson and Rosenberg. In addition to taking "appropriate administrative action" against the two professors, BLSA said, the administration should bar them from teaching any of the mandatory first-year classes.

The official reprimands of Nesson and Rosenberg, further-more, should be published in the *Harvard Crimson,* the university's student newspaper, and the *Harvard Law Bulletin,* an alumni periodical.

The multicultural bureaucracy at the law school needed to be expanded as well. BLSA demanded that the school create an Office of Multicultural Affairs. Mandatory sensitivity training should be instituted for all incoming students, as well as faculty and administrators.

One demand would spark national interest. BLSA declared that the law school must draw up and impose policies that would formally prohibit racial harassment—that is, institute a speech code. One female member of BLSA, Lacey Schwartz, publicly defended this last demand as necessary for combating "an institutional climate of apathy and complicity in issues of racial insensitivity and harassment."

BLSA and its supporters organized a rally to punctuate their demands. They selected Monday, April 15 for the gathering. Known to most Americans as Tax Day, the date was notable at Harvard Law School mostly because it was one of two days on which the school would host students admitted to the next fall's entering class. In other words, this was a day when the administration would take special pains to make a good impression on incoming students. BLSA understood, in turn, that this date offered a prime opportunity to embarrass the administration.

In the warming chill of a spring morning in New England, a crowd gathered outside Harkness Commons to rally against the racial events of the season. The rally was scheduled to begin at 11:30, twenty minutes before most classes were to adjourn. The organizers timed the event to disrupt classes by prompting sympathetic students to rise and leave the classrooms at the stated time in a noisy shuffle. Most professors learned of the gambit beforehand, and some took preemptive action, such as ending class early for the day. Other, more senior professors, unaware of the scheduled extracurricular activities, seemed mystified as participating students took leave en masse at the appointed hour.

More than three hundred students attended the rally outside Harkness Commons. Although students came from throughout the university, most were law students—a massive gathering that reflected both the shared outrage at the acts of Kiwi Camara and Matthias Scholl, and the leftist sensibilities of the student population. BLSA representatives delivered speeches denouncing the recent acts as intolerable, as well as suggesting that the law school was infected by systemic bias. The entire administration attended the rally, lending it an official air as they took their punishment. Deans Robert Clark, Todd Rakoff and Suzanne Richardson all were on hand to show support.

After a few speeches, the gathering turned into a silent protest as the assembled formed long lines in a show of solidarity. Protesters queued up on both sides of the sidewalks that traversed the campus; the human lines wound from Harkness Commons ("the Hark") to Pound Hall and back around to alongside Langdell Hall and the library. One observer described the scene as suggestive of a gauntlet that nonprotesting students had to run in order to enter the besieged buildings. Ironically, one student who happened upon the event and seemed oblivious to the commotion was Kiwi Camara. He walked through the lines of students blocking the entrance to the Hark, stepped through the dual lines of defense, and then entered the building. Observers saw it as a sort of metaphor for naiveté breaching the walls of political correctness.

Two of the better-known members of this ideological conga line were nationally prominent African-American professors. One was Cornel West, one of fourteen instructors designated as University Professors at Harvard and the most famous member of Harvard's Afro-American Studies Department. The other was Charles Ogletree, who two years earlier had been ranked by the *National Law Journal* as one of the one hundred most influential lawyers in America.

Cornel West, dressed for the rally in a dapper if dated three-piece suit, was a man whose published work exuded self-love. Born in Oklahoma and raised by a family of black preachers, West would note typically in one of his books that "the legendary 'free mind' of black Oklahomans associated ... with such black natives as Ralph Ellison, John Hope Franklin, Charlie Christian, the Gap Band, and, I humbly add, myself." He believed his upbringing had bestowed upon him exemplary "existential and ethical equipment" for life: "The three major components of this equipment were a Christian ethic of love-informed service to others, ego-deflating humility about oneself owing to the precious yet fallible humanity of others, and politically engaged struggle for social betterment."

In fact, West would demonstrate little such ego-deflation in his career and writings. He wrote that he "arrived at Princeton's philosophy department—by far the best in the country at the time"—fortified with Marxism he had picked up while a student at Harvard College. His self-described "modern artistic soul mates" were such miscellaneous luminaries as musician John Coltrane, writers Samuel Beckett and Toni Morrison, playwright Tennessee Williams, "and above all Anton Chekhov." He later offered that his arrest and jailing at Yale in 1984, as part of an unlawful protest for greater unionization, "served as a fine example for my wonderful son, Clifton," then approaching adolescence. West once complained that after leaving his "rather elegant" car in a safe parking lot in Manhattan to take a taxi up to Harlem, his "blood began to boil" as he experienced trouble in getting a taxi driver to take him there—this after he admitted parking his car many blocks south to avoid endangering his own property.

He would describe himself as a "prophetic Christian freedom fighter" who sought to reconcile the Christianity of his youth with the atheistic Marxism and leftism of his adulthood. He further viewed himself as a "modern Christian person of African descent in America trying to love my way through the darkness of an advanced capitalist global system and the thunder of postmodern market-driven culture." An overriding goal he carried to Harvard was "defending sophisticated Marxist theory as an indispensable—though by itself inadequate—intellectual weapon in the struggle for individuality and democracy." The fall of the Iron Curtain did not daunt him in this task. In his 1991 book, *The Ethical Dimensions of Marxist Thought,* West argued, "One of the major ironies of our time is that Marxist thought becomes even more relevant after the collapse of communism in the Soviet Union and Eastern Europe than it was before." He reasoned that the triumph of capitalism was now globally unchecked and therefore far more dangerous. (Left unanswered was how Marxism could be more relevant given that it had collapsed due to its own impracticability and lack of popular appeal.)

West amassed a modest following among undergraduates, but the larger intellectual community was not impressed. In a devastating survey of West's life work, Leon Wieseltier, writing for the left-of-center *New Republic,* appraised West's books as "almost completely worthless." His writings, Wieseltier continued, were "an endless exercise in misplaced Marxism" as well as "monuments to the devastation of a mind by the squalls of theory": "noisy, tedious, slippery ... sectarian, humorless, pedantic and self-endeared."

As if to alleviate this problem through sheer attrition, West, once ensconced at Harvard, did not write a new academic book for over a decade. This led the notoriously irascible new president of Harvard University, Lawrence Summers, to confront him in early 2002 about the current state of his scholarship. Prior to serving as U.S. treasury secretary in the Clinton administration, Summers had been a member of the Economics Department at Harvard. As president of the university, he lost little time in alienating his new subordinates. (He told one professor at the law school that a question she had posed to him was "stupid." He later apologized to her.)

Summers noted that West had found time to record a rap CD and serve as an advisor to Al Sharpton in his nascent presidential campaign, but not to write academic works. This enraged West, who charged that Summers had "disrespected" him. Summers leveled these accusations, West complained, even though he "hadn't listened to a note of my CD." West also pulled out his trump card, claiming in an interview on Black Entertainment Television that Summers' actions reflected a fear that "the Negroes are taking over." A subsequent apology from Summers did not alter West's plans to decamp from Harvard *à la* Derrick Bell. Noting that the provost of Princeton had called him almost every week after surgery for prostate cancer (as opposed to Summers, who did not send him a get-well card until two months after the operation), West announced that he would be leaving Harvard for Princeton at the end of the 2002 academic year. This widely publicized, bitter exchange rocked Harvard just as the speech-code controversy was reverberating throughout the law school.

Standing alongside West at the speech-code rally was his "spokesman" in the controversy with Summers, Professor Charles Ogletree. A tall black man with receding hairline and full moustache, Ogletree sported a sharp-looking double-breasted suit and a stellar reputation. He did not earn a mention by West along with Coltrane and Tennessee Williams as one of his "soul mates," but he surely meshed with West's politics as well as anybody at Harvard. While West would shake up the university with his sundry personal demands, Ogletree concentrated his fire on opponents of leftism outside Cambridge.

In the escalating race crisis at Harvard Law School, Ogletree was the one faculty member who, more than any other, gave his blessing to the student activists protesting for a speech code. Derrick Bell wrote that after his departure from Harvard, Ogletree "assumed much of my role of working with minority students at the Law School." This was his natural role, for Ogletree had arrived at Harvard Law an agent of racial controversy, and had quickly become the school's best-known advocate of far-left race-related causes. During the fall of 2001, he had made national news by spearheading the campaign to make the U.S. government pay reparations to African-Americans for slavery. Ogletree had then attended the United Nations World Conference against Racism—a parley boycotted by the Bush administration—where Third World nations made the call for slavery reparations a global one. Ogletree served as the co-chairman of the Reparations Coordinating Committee, a collection of attorneys and allies preparing to bring suit against the federal government and other entities seeking reparations for descendants of African slaves.

Ogletree based his case for reparations on an alleged "breach of contract" between newly emancipated slaves and the federal government following the Civil War. That there was in fact no such contract by any reasonable legal construction did not deter him and his band from plotting lawsuits that, he predicted, "could amount to trillions of dollars." He noted in an article published later in 2002, "We have spent the last two years engaged in legal research and identifying a number of potential defendants such as government entities, corporations and private institutions." His initial survey of potential deep-pocket defendants had gone well enough for him to announce, "I've embraced reparations as the most important work of my legal career."

That was saying a great deal, for Ogletree had been prominent in a number of high-profile left-wing causes. Prior to receiving tenure in 1993, he had been known not so much for his scholarship as for his criminal defense work and radical politics. He had helped raise money to defend black communist Angela Davis in her 1972 murder trial. During the Senate confirmation hearings for Clarence Thomas's nomination to the Supreme Court, Ogletree had represented Anita Hill. This undertaking took on the trappings of criminal defense as Hill faced credible charges of perjury from a member of the Senate Judiciary Committee, Arlen Specter.

Further controversy dogged Ogletree when he sought tenure in the early 1990s. When he tried to publish an article in the *Harvard Law Review* to bolster his chances, rumors surfaced that editors at the *Review* ghostwrote it for him. In fact, the editors merely overhauled Ogletree's tenure piece to make it publishable after he had missed several deadlines.

Ogletree's personal style may have been slightly lower key than Derrick Bell's, but his views on race and law were every bit as radical. A onetime public defender and criminal defense lawyer in Washington D.C., Ogletree regarded the

criminal justice system as imbued with deep-seated racial prejudice. "As it happens," he wrote, "the point is precisely that
much of the enforcement of the criminal law is irrational; it is
not reason but racial animus which motivates many of the practices adopted by the criminal justice system." Criminals could
not rightly be held individually responsible for their offenses:
"law-and-order advocates abdicate responsibility by charac-
terizing criminality as an individual failing that can be com-
bated using traditional forms of punishment." Rather, "crime
demonstrates a failure of community" that is best addressed
through "rehabilitation, not just of the criminal, but of the com-
munity-society itself."

Several years before demands would flare up at Harvard
for a racial harassment code, Ogletree had already laid out an
intellectual basis for such an undertaking. He made this argument in an article in the *Gonzaga Law Review* entitled "The
Limits of Hate Speech: Does Race Matter?" It certainly does,
according to Ogletree, as different races have entirely different conceptions of what constitutes free speech. "African Americans experience free speech from a different perspective than
white Americans," he argued. As a result, "racial minorities
often have a different sense of the importance of First Amendment rights to the political process," as "minorities have been
consistently prevented from participating in public expression."

What is the result of these clashing conceptions of liberty? "The upshot of this argument is that free speech is not
fundamental to the liberty of minorities," Ogletree asserted in
an eye-catching sentence. This is because "Liberty has been
protected by equality, not by the freedom to speak." Throughout his analysis, Ogletree ignored the degree to which racial
equality was a direct consequence of freedom of speech—
namely, the many books, tracts and articles written by

abolitionists that culminated in Lincoln's Emancipation Proclamation, the Civil War Amendments to the Constitution, and the Civil Rights Act.

Ogletree was shrewd enough as an inside player at Harvard Law to realize that an outright embrace of speech codes on campuses would undermine his standing among key professors opposed to such restrictions. He backed away from advocating racial speech codes expressly. Instead of codes, Ogletree urged government to honor its "affirmative moral duty to mitigate the harms of hate speech, by enforcing affirmative action policies, providing affordable housing for minorities, or engaging in programs of education."

Ogletree's students would be neither as strained in their analysis nor as circumspect in their approach. They would carry forward his reasoning—and the theories espoused by other affiliated scholars—to its logical conclusion, making demands that would undermine basic constitutional freedoms. While Ogletree would not publicly endorse these demands, he offered the students both sympathy and intellectual cover for their protests.

WATCHING THESE DEVELOPMENTS with intense interest was the man at the vortex of the controversy, Dean Robert Clark. A blue-eyed man of average height, shorn of a well-groomed red beard he had worn prior to his selection as dean, Clark was a diffident intellectual who flinched from the sharp ideological jousting that was a vital part of his job. He had begun his deanship tarred with the label "conservative"; it was a misnomer, but it would help determine the role he played in the Camara controversy.

Raised in New Orleans, the second of nine children, Clark grew up in a traditional Roman Catholic home. At one point he decided to join the Maryknoll Society and commenced studies to become a priest. He later dropped out of the seminary, however, his faith being, in his words, a casualty of "too much philosophy."

Clark enrolled at Columbia University to study full-time the philosophy that had killed his prior career interest. Then he went to Harvard for his law degree. After excelling there, Clark chose a career in academia, first joining the faculty at Yale Law School, then returning to his alma mater. At Harvard, Clark taught corporations law and developed a reputation as a leading intellectual force in the field. He supplemented his income handsomely by serving as counsel and consultant to outside businesses.

Clark likely would have remained a law professor with a reputation restricted to academia and certain business circles had he not, in 1985, injected himself into the principal philosophical tug-of-war then under way at the law school. In May of that year, Clark spoke to the Harvard Club of New York City at a debate hosted by the Federalist Society. A national group of conservative and libertarian students and attorneys, the Federalist Society had held this weekend symposium to discuss what it termed "a growing crisis in the American legal system." Of particular concern was the "neo-Marxist" Critical Legal Studies movement and its attempt "to effect a revolutionary 'utopian' change in American society."

In his remarks, Clark threw in his lot with the liberal traditionalists at Harvard who were opposing the pugnacious Crits. He took on the Crits for advancing a militant and sloppily constructed legal philosophy, one that he believed boiled down in practice to merely a "ritual slaying of the elders." He faulted the Crits for undermining the historically high standards of scholarship at the law school. The Crits also had demonstrated a "knee-jerk bias against business ... and the legal profession, something nihilistic" which threatened both Harvard and America.

In a subsequent interview, Clark also spoke up in defense of Harvard's decision not to award tenure to two Crits, Clare Dalton and David Trubek, in 1987. He told one national publication, "This place has become crazy to work at," and condemned the two Crits for mediocre teaching skills and lack of "publishing excellence."

Clark's willingness to decry publicly the baleful trends at Harvard earned him the attention of national publications and figures. Although Clark was not a conservative, a number of conservative observers applauded him for at least holding the line against Marxist-inspired philosophy. Moreover, his defense of traditional legal scholarship gained him the good will of the wealthy alumni and corporate donors on whose support the law school depended for continued preeminence. In 1989, as the law school became ever more embroiled in seemingly inexhaustible controversies over race and sex in faculty hiring, Dean James Vorenberg announced his resignation. The well-positioned Clark was then picked to be his successor.

The left at Harvard reacted violently. Morton Horwitz, a leading Crit, termed Clark's selection an "outrageous appointment" and maintained that Clark had "regularly opposed minorities, women, and people with different views than his."

At first, Clark described himself as a "traditionalist" and even governed that way for a while. He tried to exert more control over the increasingly fractious faculty by centralizing decision-making. He placed himself at the head of the school's appointments committee, and came out against giving tenure to Charles Ogletree (explaining that Ogletree, while a noted litigator, was not a scholar). He proposed eliminating the office of public-interest counseling. Since few if any Harvard Law students needed any sort of formal "counseling" on how to figure out what to do with their careers, this office was a notorious boondoggle that served mostly to encourage students to work pro bono for left-wing lobbies and social causes after graduation. Clark also suggested modest budget cuts for half a dozen clinical programs.

Clark's efforts to pare back the bureaucracy ran into a brick wall, and Clark eventually reversed himself on all these proposals. From this, the left learned that he did not have the stomach for real reform if it involved sustained ideological combat. As one liberal author observed with discernible satisfaction, "Clark backpedaled on almost every politically incorrect action he took."

Instead of trimming the school's bureaucracy, Clark shifted course, trying to atone for his earlier proposals. He worked to establish two new public-interest law scholarships. He secured new funding for the loan repayment program, which helped students who chose a career in "public interest" work to repay their loans. In practice, this program effectively subsidized left-of-center, self-styled "public interest" lobbies such as the American Civil Liberties Union by sending them recruits from recent Harvard Law graduates. Clark oversaw construction of a new building to house the school's legal services programs. He also endorsed Ogletree's application for tenure.

Clark's response to the Frug-*Revue* controversy of 1992 was further confirmation of his evolution from traditionalist liberal to pliable dean. This crisis, in the judgment of Professor Alan Dershowitz, touched off the "most recent cycle" of attacks on free speech at Harvard. This cycle would culminate in the call for a racial harassment code ten years later.

In January 1992, editors of the *Harvard Law Review* considered whether to publish an article submitted by Mary Joe Frug. The wife of Harvard Law professor Jerry Frug, she had worked as a law professor at the nearby New England School of Law, where she was known for her outspoken feminism and support for Critical Legal Studies. Both Frugs were leftist heroes at Harvard. During Derrick Bell's sit-in over the denial of tenure to Clare Dalton in 1987, the Frugs had brought dinner to his office. In the spring of 1992, while Mary Joe was walking outside her home in Cambridge, an unknown assailant brutally murdered her. She left behind her uncompleted and controversial article.

Editors of the *Review* were deeply divided over whether to publish Frug's article. Despite the natural sympathies aroused by such a tragedy, her allies on the *Review* found that her article was not an easy sell. Like many Crit works, the piece did not follow the accepted rules of legal scholarship. Citing the pop singer Madonna, it alternated between a celebration of sexual liberation and invective against the "terror" that comes from living under a culture of male oppression. (Frug never commented on the possible relationship between these two facets of culture.) The article also was full of raw profanity. "We are raped at work or on route to work because of our sex, because we are cunts," Frug declared at one point, with typical bluntness. In 1992, the editors of the *Review* voted to publish the article.

"A Postmodern Feminist Legal Manifesto (An Unfinished Draft)" would achieve for Frug a level of renown in legal circles she had not enjoyed in life. When in 1999 a law professor compiled a list of the "Top Ten Politically Correct Law Review Articles" for the *Florida State University Law Review,* Frug's posthumous article was selected as number one. (Articles by

Duncan Kennedy and Derrick Bell also made the list, so Harvard Law accounted for fully 30 percent of the total.) The article also signaled that the *Harvard Law Review* was wandering further from traditional standards for legal scholarship after serving for decades as an informal custodian of such traditions for the nation's law schools. The *Review,* for example, had begun, perpetuated and published the *Bluebook* in conjunction with several other law schools. Subtitled *A Uniform System of Citation,* the *Bluebook* literally set the standards for all law reviews and legal scholars in the nation, prescribing the definitive rules for proper citation of authorities in legal documents and law journals. Now, for the sake of scoring certain ideological points, the editors of the *Review* had undercut the prestige of their journal by publishing Frug's crude polemic.

Dissenting editors on the *Review* soon retaliated, and their offensive method of protest would become as infamous as the Frug article itself. In the annual April Fool's Day parody issue of the publication, known as the *Harvard Law Revue,* these editors, mostly conservative, published a spoof of the Frug article, mocking its stream-of-consciousness writing style and vulgarities. Presented at the *Harvard Law Review*'s annual banquet, the parody was entitled "He-Manifesto of Post-Mortem Legal Feminism," with Mary Joe Frug denoted as "Rigor-Mortis Professor of Law."

Leftists at Harvard Law pounced on this extraordinary insensitivity. Their first impulse was predictable: they lashed out at campus conservatives, or at least the closest thing to conservatives they could find at the institution.

One of their first actions was invading the office of Professor Charles Fried, a tall, angular man who in intellect, speech and bearing strongly suggested a nineteenth-century diplomat. Six feet, three inches tall, with thin, graying hair atop round glasses and tweed sport coats, Fried was the nearest semblance of a conservative on the Harvard Law faculty. Fried and his family fled Prague in 1939 before the advancing Nazis, and emigrated to New York. Henceforth Fried carried with him a lifelong aversion to totalitarianism. After a stellar academic career capped off by a clerkship for Justice John Harlan, Fried joined the Harvard Law faculty in 1961. He carved out specialties in contracts, legal philosophy and constitutional law.

A self-described "Czech Jew" wary of governmental encroachments on individual autonomy, Fried found common cause in Ronald Reagan's vision of limited government. He explained that he came to "share Reagan's gut-level dislike for the pretensions of government in general." For the same reason, he concurred with Reagan's opposition to racial quotas and government-endorsed racial preferences, practices he believed were an attempt to impose "a collectivist conception of equality that had no warrant in the Constitution, the civil-rights laws, or our traditions as a society."

Fried's legal theories rejected the relativism ascendant throughout the academy. In his book *Contract As Promise,* he argued that a foundation of basic ethical principles underlay all contract law: "At the level of theory I hope to show that the law of contract does have an underlying, unifying structure, and at the level of doctrinal exposition I hope to show that that structure can be referred to moral principles." Though he personally supported abortion rights, Fried thought *Roe v. Wade* "a symptom of a mistaken approach to judging, an approach that confused and threatened the ideal of the rule of law" by settling important social disputes through judicial decree instead of debate in democratic assemblies.

By his own insistence, Fried was not a conservative, but rather a "19th-century liberal." A freethinker and an agnostic, he took pains in his writings and work to distinguish himself from the faction he termed the "hard right." Appointed to the Massachusetts Supreme Judicial Court by a Republican governor, Fried infuriated conservatives in 1997 with his majority opinion in the Fells Acre Day School case. This case became a national cause célèbre after the owners of a Massachusetts day care center and one of their workers were convicted on mass child abuse counts in trials that relied on highly questionable interrogations of the allegedly victimized children. In his opinion in *Commonwealth v. Amirault,* Fried overturned a lower court's order granting a new trial to one of the defendants because, he stated, a new trial would undermine the courts' interest in "finality." In 2003, the U.S. Supreme Court cited Fried's writings in support of its decision in *Lawrence v. Texas,* which held that the Constitution guarantees a right to engage in homosexual intercourse.

Fried was his own man. His warm personality drew students to his classes, including many who were politically left of center. He served as the faculty advisor to the Harvard chapter of the conservative/libertarian Federalist Society. He was open-minded and tolerant of dissent, expressing his views in class politely and demanding that his students do the same. Fried was also one of the very few professors known to invite his classes to his home for cocktail receptions.

The left had never forgiven Fried for his criticism of Derrick Bell and the protests related to his faculty battles. Fried contended that Bell's overriding purpose throughout these squabbles was "to make a martyr of himself and preen," and noted that Bell's tactics of urging students to violate rules were "not admirable." Fried grew angry simply talking to Bell; in one conversation, Fried reiterated his own opposition to racial quotas but acknowledged that Bell might have to support such policies, as a practical matter, to placate his "constituency." It was a blunt assertion that still rankled Bell years later.

Fried had served as U.S. solicitor general in the Reagan administration and was known as the only Republican on the Harvard Law faculty. While he personally eschewed the label "conservative" (presumably at least in part out of professional self-defense), Fried was, if by default, an unofficial mentor to the school's conservative students. He was a natural first target when the campus left sought to vent its wrath.

"Hello. Can I help you?" Fried replied as protesters entered his office. They promptly sat down and made themselves at home, offering no response other than holding up a sign that read, "Don't talk to us, talk to Dean Clark." Fried called the dean's office and demanded that they be removed. Not until Fried threatened to contact the bar authorities in the states where the students were applying to practice law did they finally leave.

The following day, the protesters entered the office of Reinier Kraakman, a corporations professor. Kraakman avoided confrontation by abandoning his office, saying he needed to leave for class anyhow. The protesters stayed a half-hour longer, then departed.

Aware of the threat to basic order at the school that such actions posed if the administration failed to respond, Fried pressed Dean Clark to initiate disciplinary measures against the protesters, who became known as the "Fried Four." As the confrontation escalated, students wearing masks blocked the door to the dean's office in Griswold Hall. At one point, they turned Fried away when he sought to pass.

The conflict was a moment of decision for Clark. As the controversy swelled, fifteen professors—including Duncan Kennedy, Christopher Edley, Frank Michelman, Martha Field,

Elizabeth Bartholet and Charles Nesson—signed a letter demanding Clark's resignation. The letter also demanded changes in the appointments committee, alleging that the school still was not hiring enough women and minorities, and called on the president of the university, Neil Rudenstein, to investigate the Frug-*Revue* matter. Dominating this group of fifteen professors (a bloc that constituted more than one-fourth of the faculty) were the Crits, who saw this as an opportunity to drive the new "conservative" dean out of power.

One of these professors, David Kennedy, brought a formal complaint against the students who authored the *Revue* parody article. He claimed that this act constituted harassment and was akin to sexual assault. Harvey Silverglate, a Harvard alumnus and civil rights attorney in the Boston area, would later observe of the *Revue* piece: "It was a moronic, tasteless, cruel piece of writing that nonetheless qualified as parody." The law professors making these extreme demands surely knew this, as well as the fact that, as Silverglate pointed out, the First Amendment would have fully protected the authors if Harvard Law School were a public institution. Yet the left pressed its advantage.

The principle at stake in this controversy—basic freedom of speech—was also not lost on Dean Clark. The law-review editors who authored the parody had acted foolishly, and were of a piece with Kiwi Camara and Matthias Scholl in their e-mails a decade later. In response, however, the campus left had trespassed in professors' offices, disrupted the everyday functions of the law school, and fired off a list of unreasonable and borderline unconstitutional demands of the administration. Still, even with the lines drawn so clearly and outrageously, Clark caved.

The school refused to discipline the students who had violated the rules. The administrative board reviewing the trespassing incidents announced it would not bring charges against the three identified members of the Fried Four. Nor would the masked protesters who blocked the hallway to the dean's office receive any sanction beyond a warning. When it came to the *Revue* parody, however, Clark took far broader measures. He proposed creating entirely new rules to prevent a repetition of such an act. Because there were no rules in place to allow for punishing the student authors, Clark formed a committee and commissioned it to write a sexual harassment code.

Harvey Silverglate wrote to Clark to protest this action. Clark responded that such a committee and mission were necessary. "This discussion is a sign of the times, as is the need perceived among students that we have to discuss this or be seen as uncaring of their concerns," Clark replied—a remarkable admission that his actions were driven by public relations rather than regard for civil liberties.

Silverglate had kept an eye on his alma mater since graduating in 1967. Over the years, he had represented more than two hundred Harvard students and a dozen faculty members involved in disciplinary or other disputes at the university. He also co-authored a well-received book about political correctness on American campuses, *The Shadow University.* "I consider myself part of the left," said Silverglate, but in Clark's reaction to both the Frug-*Revue* crisis and, years later, the call for a racial harassment code, he saw a dean betraying liberalism by his unwillingness to defend the First Amendment.

Clark's response to the Frug-*Revue* controversy was a prologue to his actions ten years later after Kiwi Camara sent his fateful e-mail. In both cases, the common thread was a retreat from basic civil rights to appease campus protesters and lower the noise of the moment. This tendency to follow the path of least ideological resistance would result in a steady, decade-long decline in civil liberties at Harvard on Clark's watch, a development that would lead Silverglate and others to denounce the dean for cowardice and lack of principle. Along the way, Harvard Law School would evolve from a redoubt of freedom—where every rhetorical right a free nation could bestow on a citizen was exercised freely and vigorously— to an institution where such essential freedoms were more endangered than in the rest of society. Silverglate would note that through all of this, one of the most important underlying developments was "the transformation of Bob Clark from a principled law professor to an unprincipled administrator."

IT TOOK ONLY A WEEK for the administration to swing into full damage-control mode after the April 15 speech-code rally. On April 22, Clark and his two subordinate deans, Todd Rakoff, dean of the J.D. program, and Suzanne Richardson, dean of students, sent out an e-mail to students, faculty and staff. "Some appalling things have happened at Harvard Law School recently," the message began. These included that "a first-year student anonymously posted on a Web site run by a student organization his course outline, parts of which used language conveying an attitude of contempt for African-Americans." Scholl's e-mail and the swastika flyers also were mentioned. "We emphatically condemn these acts as contrary to both the spirit and the mission of the Harvard Law School."

Clark then went beyond denunciation of the individual offenders to propose several sweeping changes. The administration pledged to meet with representatives of the Black Law Students Association (BLSA) on May 8 and consult with them on how to respond properly to the recent race-related developments. "Following the excellent suggestion of certain faculty members (Professors Ogletree, Edley, Guinier, Mack, and Wilkins) . . . several summer faculty workshops will be devoted to exploring and developing a set of institutional mechanisms that can both anticipate and defuse racially offensive incidents and help improve pedagogy regarding sensitive cleavage lines in our society."

Clark also established a committee along these lines. Calling it the "Committee on Healthy Diversity," he stated that it would be composed of faculty, students and staff. Among other things, the committee would debate whether "the faculty should develop a racial harassment policy."

The Committee on Healthy Diversity bore an Orwellian name and presumably a similarly authoritarian orientation. The term "racial harassment policy" was obviously a synonym for "speech code." In stating that he would be following the "excellent suggestion" of some of the school's most far-left professors in instituting various faculty workshops, Clark was, in effect, making the Crit-dominated left an arbiter of school policy. Moreover, the dean had gone on record as being willing, in essence, to acknowledge the "nonnegotiable" demands of a student organization, BLSA. This concession harked back to the heady, activist days of the Vietnam War.

The administration consulted school policies to determine if any of them would authorize taking formal action against Camara and Scholl. The answer was no, due to the lack of an existing speech code. Clark implicitly reprimanded Scholl, however, in a public statement about the matter. "We have a policy that e-mails should not be anonymous," Clark said, referring to the gcrocodile e-mail. In April 2002, after Scholl was referred to a law-school administrative board, Dean Rakoff repeated to the *Harvard Law Record* that disciplinary action against Scholl was "still under consideration."

Observer Harvey Silverglate judged the administration's reaction to these incidents "appalling." Regarding Camara, he observed, "He did not mean any insult. The irony is, he's what would be called at Harvard a 'person of color.' ... It was a clumsy use of language." As for Scholl, he "showed infantile judgment, but he was perfectly protected in what he did.... I think he made an intelligent point in an infantile manner."

There was also a constitutional right to disseminate anonymous e-mails. In 1995, the Supreme Court had recognized a right to anonymous speech in *McIntyre v. Ohio Elections Commission.* As in the Frug-*Revue* controversy, Silverglate noted, had this dispute occurred at a public institution, Scholl's right to transmit the e-mail—however offensive the actual note was—would have enjoyed clear constitutional protection.

As law professors at Harvard and elsewhere had long noted, it was a truism of constitutional law that the people who pressed the boundaries of the First Amendment were almost invariably obnoxious and offensive people. Now that the same phenomenon was occurring at Harvard, however, professors and students who otherwise professed to be absolutist defenders of free speech had shifted position. Clark's flip-flop was the most dramatic of all. A man who had risen to the deanship largely because of his praise of traditional notions of excellence and open discourse, Clark took the route of political expediency: creating a committee to study the controversy and tossing other vaguely leftist measures to his predominantly leftist constituents. The committee was handed a mission that put it on a collision course with the Constitution. In response, Silverglate could only describe Clark as a "gutless wonder."

Clark did his best to avoid public comment on the controversy and subsequent work of the committee. When he did speak, he used calculated, ambivalent language. Even as he charged the new Committee on Healthy Diversity with considering a speech code, he expressed simultaneously, through a spokesman, his "grave reservations" about such a code. At its moment of greatest intellectual and political crisis, Harvard Law School had become an institution without a leader.

CHAPTER FIVE

TRIUMPH OF THE CRITS

The Crits and their allies on the left, watchful for an opportunity to expand their influence at Harvard Law, saw a grand one indeed in the missteps of Professors Charles Nesson and David Rosenberg. Both professors were now vulnerable to professional censure and possibly ripe for outright replacement in the classroom. Although it was not possible to revoke their tenure and oust them from the school, they could be neutralized as effective professors.

By late March 2002, Nesson recognized that his reputation as a likeable free spirit and reliable white liberal was insufficient to save him from the racial tempest now blowing about him. So he began a campaign of apologies. He insisted that he had meant no offense and was sorry he had caused any. His suggestion that the class conduct a mock trial of Matthias Scholl may have been a legitimate "pedagogic moment," but he said that in retrospect he regretted proposing the idea.

Nesson's apologies and his prior public service to the civil rights movement did not generate enough racial good will to shield him from blowback. In April, Dean Todd Rakoff summoned Nesson to a meeting. The topic of discussion was the mock trial incident and related controversy. A liberal anxious to dodge the same race-related invective being hurled at

Nesson, Rakoff made a proposal: Would not Nesson and the law school be better off if Nesson surrendered his torts class to another professor? Nesson's replacement could teach the course through the end of the semester, after Nesson returned for a final lecture to say his goodbyes.

Rakoff and Nesson would later relate conflicting versions of the meeting. Rakoff contended that Nesson offered to step aside because he concluded he "could do more for his students this way." Nesson stated that giving up his class was Rakoff's idea, and was proposed on behalf of the administration. Nesson's account was more persuasive given the totality of the facts. Both agreed that Rakoff had suggested Morton Horwitz as the professor who would take Nesson's place.

Nesson appealed to Dean Clark for some public words of support. He pleaded with Clark to make it clear that he had not been stripped of his class as a disciplinary measure. Clark refused. By late April 2002, Nesson was complaining to the press that Clark and the school would not "alter the public impression that I've been yanked."

It was true that Nesson had brought much of this trouble down on his own head, a point made by more than one of his fellow professors. One said privately, "What the administration was responding to was what it perceived as not expression of a point of view, but grossly inappropriate classroom behavior." As this professor described it, "He's marching into another professor's classroom. He did it without warning the student or the professor he was coming. . . . He did something that was unbelievably unorthodox, invading another professor's turf, a student's privacy." Nesson had behaved in a way that was "off-the-wall pedagogically" and that was "humiliating to those students and hugely disruptive to the classroom."

Nesson's prior, cavalier admissions of illegal drug use and his mercurial antics in the classroom did not help his case. Professor Charles Fried noted that "obviously the administration was worried" about Nesson's behavior *in toto*. "His problems were further flung than that [the mock trial proposal] and the students were distressed for other reasons."

Still, divesting a professor of his class assignments was a drastic and unprecedented step at Harvard. And even those who defended the administration's actions against Nesson could not bring themselves to defend the dean's handling of David Rosenberg.

Professor Rosenberg's offense was, in essence, being a curmudgeon. The worst thing that could legitimately be said of his actions that spring was that he had stated awkwardly a fair objection to Critical Legal Studies. Rosenberg later noted in a written statement (the only comments he would issue concerning the controversy), "What I criticized was strands of black scholarship—notably, black studies and its contributions to critical race theory and various other areas.... I said that this scholarship does not enhance understanding of tort theory and I stand fully behind my criticism."

Rosenberg's opponents could not point to drug abuse or zany personal behavior or enlist some other cover for taking action against him, and Rosenberg himself identified the principle at stake. The administration, he observed, "should realize that for a faculty member to be strongly criticized—and even threatened with formal sanctions—for making critical remarks about a genre of scholarship in class strikes at the very heart of academic freedom."

He would find that at Harvard, such freedom swiftly went by the boards when faculty and administrators sensed a threat to their own careers or reputations. Moreover, Rosenberg by this point had accumulated too many powerful enemies on the left. His in-class broadside against Critical Legal Studies had inflamed in one stroke both the Crits and the left-wing minority activists on campus.

By the time he made his ill-fated race-related comments in class, Rosenberg had not recovered professionally from his run-in with feminists several years earlier during the Frug-*Revue* controversy, or from his clash with the Crits following his critique of Clare Dalton's work. After Dean Clark had established the committee to impose sexual harassment guidelines, including certain restrictions on speech, Harvey Silverglate, a friend of Rosenberg's, alerted the public to these developments in an article he wrote for the *Wall Street Journal* entitled "Harvard Law Caves In to the Censors." Silverglate criticized Clark and the Harvard Law administration for instituting sexual harassment policies that, he argued, impinged on freedom of speech for students and faculty. Rosenberg wrote a letter to the editors of the *Journal* in support of Silverglate's observations, arguing that the sexual harassment speech restrictions were part of a misguided "strategy of controlled self-censorship to ward off something worse." He even compared the overreaction and resulting policies to the early stages of McCarthyism in the 1950s.

When his crisis came, Rosenberg had few friends at the law school willing to mount the ramparts for him. The first omen of Rosenberg's demise came in the form of a comment Dean Rakoff made to the *Harvard Law Record*. Rakoff stated that he expected Rosenberg to retract his comments about Critical Legal Studies. "It was clear that Rosenberg should apologize for what he said, and he agreed to do so," said Rakoff. But Rosenberg would issue no such apology, and it is highly doubtful that the proud and sullen professor ever made such a pledge.

Next the administration gave Rosenberg a modified version of the Nesson treatment. Instead of ejecting him from his torts class, the administration announced that attendance at Rosenberg's class would become optional. Henceforth, the law school would videotape his classes and make them available to his students. Any students who preferred to avoid his class could simply watch his lectures on videotape.

Predictably, attendance at Rosenberg's class fell. The student at the center of the showdown noted the drop in attendance with satisfaction. "I'm still going to classes," Tel Cary-Sadler said, "but the classroom environment has been quite uncomfortable, and there are a lot of empty seats."

The administration's humiliation of Rosenberg—like its dismissal of Nesson from his torts class—was unprecedented, and the ramifications were even more profound. Since it was impossible to conduct a class by the Socratic method via videotape, the decision to film Rosenberg's torts class effectively repealed the Socratic method for his students. This development was a cause for jubilation among the backbenchers in Rosenberg's class, who now could simply view the videotape of his lectures at their leisure. But it was deeply damaging to legal education at Harvard, undermining not only basic academic freedom but also the unique history of the school itself. Rosenberg would not teach torts at all the following academic year.

The sanctions meted out to Rosenberg also troubled many faculty members. As one self-described liberal professor saw it, both Nesson and Rosenberg had run into trouble because of "their own idiosyncratic behavior expressed as part of a dialogue on race." Of the two, this professor believed, Rosenberg was far less to blame. In his case, "There is at least a political correctness concern: How much do you tell a professor what he can and can't say and do in the classroom? ... To say that a professor can never use the term 'blacks,' it's just crazy."

Professor Alan Dershowitz also was critical of the administration's actions. Dershowitz was an avowed civil libertarian, the preferred criminal defense attorney of the stars, and a rebellious personality. He had been rebellious since he was a child. As a student at the yeshiva in his native Brooklyn, Dershowitz had questioned the rabbis repeatedly with queries such as "Why not?" He ended up being suspended from religious class for the last six months of high school for "lack of respect." His principal ultimately advised him, "You got a good mouth on you, but not much of a Jewish mind. You should become either a lawyer or a conservative rabbi."

Dershowitz attended nearby Brooklyn College before journeying to Yale Law School; he graduated first in his class and was named editor in chief of the *Yale Law Journal*. After clerking on the Supreme Court for Justice Arthur Goldberg, Dershowitz was offered a position on the Harvard Law faculty at the age of twenty-five. Three years later, he became the youngest full professor in the school's history.

Dershowitz's brilliance and ambition transcended the traditional confines of the law school. Before long, he had become not only the best-known law professor at Harvard, but one of the nation's most renowned attorneys. Americans came to recognize his bushy red hair and moustache and silver-rimmed glasses from countless television interviews, in which he appeared both as a legal authority and, just as often, as the defense attorney of record for embattled celebrities. He first rose to national prominence as the attorney for Claus von Bulow, the wealthy socialite accused (and, with Dershowitz's intervention, acquitted) of attempting to murder his heiress wife; Dershowitz's book on the case became an acclaimed movie of the same name, *Reversal of Fortune.* His roster of clients was studded with nationally infamous defendants: former heavyweight champion Mike Tyson, hotel mogul Leona Helmsley, televangelist Jim Bakker, spy Jonathan Pollard.

This focus on criminal defense work and television interviews gave ammunition to Dershowitz's envious colleagues, who noted a lack of similar commitment to academic and intellectual publications. Still, his multiple best-selling books and national stage presence helped, in the words of one appreciative student, to "keep the brand strong" by making sure that Harvard Law School remained prominently in the public eye. He "does his part for law-school recruiting," one student remarked wryly.

In September 2003, a year after the Committee on Healthy Diversity was convened, Dershowitz would face accusations of plagiarism for the first time in his meteoric career. An article by left-wing writer Alexander Cockburn, entitled "Alan Dershowitz, Plagiarist," claimed that Dershowitz had lifted large portions of material without attribution from other works for his latest best-selling book, *The Case for Israel.* Dershowitz's offering was the most prominent of several books published that season to defend what, for decades of American foreign policy, had been a notion without need of formal defense: the right of the state of Israel to exist in peace. Cockburn accused Dershowitz of compiling ideas and insights from lesser-known writers and books and passing off their intellectual work as his own. Dershowitz responded with characteristic pugnacity: "I'm coming out swinging," he told one reporter. He added regarding Cockburn, "He doesn't like that I'm a Zionist, and he doesn't like the fact that my books are on the bestseller list."

Dershowitz managed to juggle these pursuits while remaining engaged in both his class work and the daily happenings at the law school. He was vigilant in identifying incipient threats to civil liberties. A passionate defender of Jewish and Israeli causes, Dershowitz had a self-described "Holocaust mindset" that made him a scrupulous guardian of personal freedoms at Harvard. He believed the First Amendment should be interpreted broadly, and for a time wrote a column for *Penthouse* magazine.

Though a liberal, Dershowitz had soured on the campus left in the decade preceding the call for a racial harassment code. A supporter of affirmative action when it began at the law school in 1969, Dershowitz reasoned then that "the presence of some blacks in places of prestige would diffuse tensions in black ghettoes." But the rhetoric and actions of Derrick Bell were a personal turning point. Dershowitz was appalled to learn that Bell had blasted other members of the faculty as stooges who "look black and think white." This barb was presumably aimed at fellow African-American professor Randall Kennedy, whom Dershowitz respected. Dershowitz then wrote a syndicated column rebuking Bell for trying to impose "a relative uniformity of viewpoint" rather than true diversity on the Harvard Law faculty.

The Frug-*Revue* controversy further drove a wedge between Dershowitz and the hard left. When other law professors urged the administration to discipline the authors of the parody, even though they had not violated any existing law or rule of student conduct, Dershowitz saw this demand as tyrannical and the work of a mob. He denounced the fifteen-professor cabal leading this effort as akin to an "un-Harvard Activities Committee," alluding to tactics associated with the McCarthy era. "What is wrong at Harvard," he explained, "is that for too many radical professors and students, freedom of speech for those who disagree with them is 'just not their thing.'"

Periodic calls for speech codes on college campuses also troubled Dershowitz and spurred him into action. He had noticed a pattern in the wave of demands for speech codes: some abrasive student or professor would make a dumb or offensive statement, and the campus left would overreact and demand a speech code and other concessions from the administration. He observed: "Speech codes on many campuses were little more than muscle flexing by newly empowered minorities against the expression of the old guard. It was affirmative action for some speech coupled with negative reaction against other speech."

Dershowitz was no conservative. He called the impeachment of Bill Clinton "sexual McCarthyism," condemned the Supreme Court's decision in *Bush v. Gore* as "lawless," and advocated a far more restricted view of the Second Amendment than he did of the First. (While he had never owned a firearm, he once quipped in a campus debate, "I can't say that about all of my clients.") Yet in his statements and work, there was a certain intellectual integrity and evenhandedness, as he insisted that freedom of speech exist for all members of the law-school community.

Now the most famous professor at Harvard Law, Dershowitz felt at liberty to hold forth on almost any major controversy at the school. In the speech-code crisis of 2002, he found real cause for worry. He described the administration's response to the Nesson and Rosenberg incidents as "way, way overreaction." Like other members of the faculty, Dershowitz thought much of the fault in Nesson's case lay with the embattled professor. "He committed academic suicide, basically," he observed of his longtime colleague. "He fell on his own sword.... He allowed somebody else to teach his class."

Nesson, Dershowitz noted, reacted badly to the situation. "I think Charlie made a mistake by giving in. He pandered in the end. Because he didn't do anything wrong by saying, 'Let's have a mock trial. I'll defend the student.' I would've defended the student."

Dershowitz saw Rosenberg's comments in class regarding Critical Legal Studies in a very different light. "It's clear what he meant. And what he meant to say clearly is protected academic speech." Moreover, "Rosenberg doesn't think anybody's contributed much to tort theory since Oliver Wendell Holmes." Rosenberg was not criticizing all blacks; "he meant the blacks who identify themselves and the feminists who identify themselves with [Critical Legal Studies]." As for the edict that Rosenberg's lectures be videotaped, "There's no precedent, and it's ridiculous, and it's overreactive."

Making it optional for students to associate with Rosenberg, Dershowitz concluded, was a major mistake. "You don't have an option in life in a lot of areas.... David Rosenberg is one of the great teachers at Harvard Law School. I don't think anybody should miss his class." Dershowitz found the message conveyed to the student body disturbing. "We shouldn't be coddling our students. We shouldn't be pandering."

Harvey Silverglate also spoke up for his friend Rosenberg, with whom he had practiced law for a time at a Boston firm before Rosenberg joined the faculty. Silverglate described him as a consistent civil libertarian. "It was very clear he was referring to black Critical Legal Studies," Silverglate noted of the in-class remarks. "You have a professor who's making a perfectly valid point and he's being punished for it."

In his response to the Nesson and Rosenberg flaps, Dean Clark, who had gained notoriety and ascension to the deanship largely by taking aim at Critical Legal Studies, ended up confirming the dominance of Crits at the school. He replaced one insufficiently liberal professor (Nesson) with a Crit (Horwitz), and he humiliated one of the most outspoken opponents of Critical Legal Studies (Rosenberg) by making attendance of his class optional. Both actions, in Silverglate's view, were indefensible. "I think this justified canceling Robert Clark's tenure and firing him," Silverglate said bluntly. "It was a frontal assault on what Harvard Law School stands for."

The longstanding safeguards of tenure, designed to encourage creative teaching styles and robust classroom discussions, had failed at Harvard Law. Dershowitz for one was not surprised. "Tenure doesn't work," he remarked. "Faculty members for the most part are cowards. They don't want to alienate even a single student. They're all pushing for high teaching ratings, and they want to be loved by everybody."

The downfall of Professors Nesson and Rosenberg marked far more than the failure of tenure. Other instructors took note of the lesson delivered by the administration: Professors who found themselves at odds with minority organizations, even for harmless statements uttered in class, faced the real prospect of expulsion from their classes and ruination of their good names. Once this race-related dynamic took hold in the discussion over Nesson and Rosenberg, the final outcome never was much in doubt. Nesson summed up the situation by observing of the Black Law Students Association, "When you write a letter to the Deans and the Harvard Law *Record*, you look for targets. And that's where two white guys named Nesson and Rosenberg come in."

CHAPTER SIX

DIVERSITY,
HARVARD STYLE

Summer 2002 came and offered no resolution to Harvard Law School's latest, and arguably most severe, crisis. First- and second-year students left for their summer clerkships, those mutually profitable stints in which elite firms pay promising law students top dollar for doing little work—with the understanding that both parties are lining up postgraduation employment. The faculty spent the summer in similar, well-kept leisure, vacationing or researching and writing or doing the profitable consulting that in some cases amounts to income several times that of the law school's salary. When students and faculty returned in the fall, they found that the speech-code controversy, having simmered during the summer months, was coming to a boil.

On September 6, 2002, Dean Robert Clark greeted the returning flock with an e-mail updating them on the administration's work over the summer. In a memo co-authored with Deans Rakoff and Richardson, Clark announced several new developments and initiatives designed to improve campus race relations. He informed students and faculty that he had made formal appointments to the Dean's Committee on Healthy Diversity, which would consist of six faculty members, three administrators and five students. Professor Martha Field would chair the committee.

Clark also reported the creation of a new program of instruction to promote racial amity at the school. The administration was instituting a "Difficult Conversations" workshop for students that would address the recent racial friction. A new, race-oriented teaching workshop would provide greater sensitivity training for members of the faculty. Also to follow were several presentations to the law school community on the importance of smoothing over differences arising from race, religion and gender.

The most groundbreaking and provocative component of this plan of action was the Difficult Conversations program. It would be piloted that fall in several first-year sections. The stated goal of this seminar was to reduce tensions and facilitate greater sensitivity in classroom or other discussions dealing with race, gender and other delicate issues.

Professor Field was asked about the focus and likely direction of the Committee on Healthy Diversity. Her first public comments about her new assignment as committee chairman did little to dispel mounting concerns about the committee's intentions and political bent. The committee, she told the *Record,* had broad marching orders that included consideration of a formal ban on racially offensive speech. "The same thing can happen with religion and sexual orientation," she added. Field's initial comments suggested that the potential speech code could proscribe things ranging from racially insensitive remarks to comparisons among religions to disapproval of same-sex marriage.

Clark and others toying with a speech code had failed to anticipate the waves of ridicule that would soon crash upon the school after word of these proposals leaked out (thanks largely to the resourcefulness of concerned alumni such as Harvey Silverglate). The Difficult Conversations seminars attracted special scorn and animus.

As with the repeal of the Socratic method in Rosenberg's class, Harvard Law School was tampering with the basis of its own reputation in establishing the Difficult Conversations program. This attempt to discourage unpleasant classroom dialogue clashed with the school's history and traditions. Still semi-famous were Bull Warren's predictions to his first-year students that one out of three would soon wash out of the law school. There were also the film and subsequent TV series of the same name, *The Paper Chase,* which did so much to immortalize the rigorous in-class examination of students at Harvard. Such a forensic boot camp was a far cry from the sanitized commentary and dispute resolution proposed as part of the "difficult conversations" program.

Harvard Law kicked off the workshops in September following yet another "Diversity Festival." Entitled "Managing Difficult Conversations," the seminars were mandatory for three sections of 1Ls that fall. Students received lesson books so they could prepare for the sessions and follow along in class. Part of the course was unremarkable, reinforcing a general moral relativism that was already strong among the student body, the vast majority of whom were graduates of colleges and universities where such thinking was widely dispensed and accepted. Yet the course materials took this mindset to an extreme that undermined the driving purpose of the seminars, specifically, improving race relations. Reminiscent of Nietzsche's call to move "Beyond Good and Evil," the materials proclaimed that the students needed to "Move from Truth to Meaning." Students were instructed not to "argue about who's right." After all, "Difficult Conversations are not about facts.

They're about meaning, values, interpretations, and expectations."

No right, no wrong, no problem—or so Harvard's future lawyers were taught in an attempt to stamp out prejudice. They were instructed that when confronted with evil, they should first question their own attitudes and values. "When your internal voice says: 'They're wrong, stupid, stubborn, biased, oversensitive, evil …' Translate to: I wonder why they see it differently? What's their data? What's their reasoning?" Students were left to wonder what would have happened had Martin Luther King Jr. read from the same relativistic script, and whether, if he had, such interracial "difficult conversations" might never have occurred because he would not have denounced segregation as "evil."

Students and faculty alike were confused about the aim of the workshops. One student complained that the seminars were vague and meandering. "At the first session of one workshop, the conversation dealt with how to break up with your boyfriend," said Lacey Schwartz, an African-American student who was serving on both the Committee on Healthy Diversity and the Black Law Students Association. "Then the second session was about race and other things—so there was confusion about what the workshop was focused on." One member of the faculty noted that by imposing the workshops, the school was stigmatizing conflict. This was an odd posture, the professor remarked, since conflict is an essential part of the practice of law.

"Teaching students not to say what they really mean— that's a hell of a training for a lawyer," Harvey Silverglate observed. "If you can't deal with 'difficult conversations,' you should not be in law school. You should go to divinity school." When Silverglate informed Dorothy Rabinowitz, a columnist at the *Wall Street Journal,* of these developments, she exposed them in a biting commentary that did much to draw attention to the state of affairs at Harvard Law.

Silverglate recalled an incident at his thirty-fifth Harvard Law class reunion the previous summer that had foreshadowed Dean Clark's approach. By way of addressing the recent troubles at the school, Clark reassured the assembled alumni that he was working hard to improve all social relations at the school. He was not content with simply seeing good manners enforced in classroom discussions. "I want to make them [the students] like each other," Clark declared. Silverglate was incredulous. "What kind of social engineering is that?" he later asked. "They can't even make the faculty get along."

The faculty workshop on race relations received less attention. Yet even this largely meaningless exercise in saving face offered a powerful statement about who really ran the school and shaped its general approach to race relations. In announcing the forthcoming "teaching workshop" for faculty members, Clark stated that the sessions would be devoted to "exploring the best practices for effective teaching of race and gender related material, and of good teaching in diverse classrooms." There would be no more Nessons and Rosenbergs upsetting minority students with unorthodox or challenging questions or comments in class. To help ensure this outcome, Clark tapped the professor he thought best able to instruct her colleagues on proper etiquette for conducting race-oriented classroom discussions: Lani Guinier.

Guinier was the only black female professor at Harvard Law School, filling the void on the faculty that had sent Derrick Bell into exile. A graduate of Yale Law School, Guinier had worked in the Carter administration in the Civil Rights Division of the Justice Department. In 1993, President Clinton nominated her to head this same division. He withdrew the nomination shortly thereafter, following a brief skirmish with national conservatives who branded her a "quota queen." In her writings, Guinier had continued to be controversial by arguing radical positions. One was that elections in which only one candidate wins—so-called winner-takes-all elections— should be "discarded," as such practices are unfair and discriminate against minorities. Majority voting should be replaced with "cumulative voting," which would allow a certain number of top vote-getters statewide to win election to, for example, Congress. This would ensure the election of more minorities. Guinier also articulated a theory of electoral "authenticity," whereby elected officials must "'look like' or act like the voters themselves" and share "common physical or cultural traits with constituents" in order to be legitimate representatives.

Guinier was also one of the nation's most vociferous champions of racial quotas in college admissions. In one law-review article, she pointed to a study of graduates of the University of Michigan Law School that showed such graduates faring well in the workplace. She and the authors of the study concluded that this success rebutted critics of affirmative action; if these graduates had been unqualified for admission, Guinier argued, why were they now prospering in their legal careers? She added that "hard," test-based admissions criteria were not better at predicting success than "soft," affirmative-action criteria that included a person's race. Guinier urged law schools not simply to retrench, but to "expand their practice" of admitting students by race and move toward a completely "soft" admissions policy that downplayed grades and test scores. Guinier believed the nation's universities must "revamp the entire admissions criteria for *all* incoming students."

Critics would note that this defense of affirmative action was an exercise in circular reasoning. That these graduates did not fail upon graduation did not mean they were as qualified as white applicants who were rejected for admission. Rather, admission to a prestigious law school was what gave a person entrée to the career opportunities that allowed these graduates to excel in law; the "spoils" in the "spoils system" were the admissions themselves. Yet Guinier concluded somewhat self-righteously, "If a school wishes to choose students who will have successful legal careers, true to the spirit of a publicly funded university, affirmative-action-type admission processes are far superior to generic test-based ones." Moreover, "affirmative action critics' much-touted reliance on objective measures of merit has little to recommend them over the life span of a lawyer."

That the author of such views was designated as Harvard's official authority on discussing racial issues was significant. Given the penalties meted out to Professors Nesson and Rosenberg, any "sensitivity training" could only send a message to the faculty to watch their words. With Guinier and company running the show, it became clear that the safest professional course was to express approval for affirmative action and other racial preferences. The next-safest course was to say nothing at all.

THE COMMITTEE ON HEALTHY DIVERSITY offered an array of individuals demonstrating intellectual diversity as Harvard understood it: the members subscribed to viewpoints ranging from left to far left. The collection of liberals and leftists on the committee was a fascinating mélange of personalities and prominent theorists in law, and a representative sample of what Harvard Law School stood for.

Professor Martha Field, the committee's chairman, was well suited to her new role insofar as her ardent liberalism reflected the panel's philosophical center. A pleasant, voluble woman with often-disheveled hair and absent-minded tendencies (her office was a veritable swirl of scattered paper and boxes), Field would reveal herself, in her work and leadership of the committee, as someone genuinely torn between concern for civil liberties and sensitivity toward those complaining of racial mistreatment at the school.

One of her more important law-review articles had argued that, contrary to the analysis offered in *Roe v. Wade,* the courts should locate the constitutional right to abortion not in the "penumbra" among the various amendments in the Bill of Rights, but in the First Amendment. The right of free speech, she reasoned, "encompasses choices about how to live, how to look, what to wear, whom to live with, how to develop one's personality."

Field believed that the First Amendment's establishment clause provided other grounds for striking down anti-abortion legislation. The establishment clause, which prohibits the government from establishing an official church or religion, similarly forbids anti-abortion legislation, she argued, because such laws constitute an "establishment of religion." The *reductio ad absurdum* of Field's reasoning was that any law based on moral or religious premises could conceivably constitute an unconstitutional establishment of religion—even laws against murder, slavery or segregation. Put another way, the First Amendment virtually prohibited law itself.

With such abuse of the First Amendment accepted as "scholarship," it was no wonder that free speech was on the defensive at Harvard. Yet this radical reasoning was rather typical for a member of the faculty. On this committee, at this school, Field was a centrist.

No less liberal, if more rigorous in his thought, was the most famous member of the committee, Alan Dershowitz. One fellow professor and committee member described him as representing "ballast" for the committee. All agreed that Dershowitz's presence helped ensure that the committee would show proper deference to civil liberties. Dershowitz would not shy from using the committee as a platform for promoting himself and the liberal principles for which he had fought throughout his career.

One of Dershowitz's best friends on the faculty also would assume a prominent role in the Committee on Healthy Diversity. Frank Michelman was as reserved as Dershowitz was flamboyant. A tall, introverted man with a salt-and-pepper moustache, Michelman had an easy and likable manner that had earned him many friends among his colleagues. He gained the enduring good will of the school's Crits by siding with Derrick Bell during his standoff with the administration. Michelman intervened in the dispute by lobbying Harvard University president Neil Rudenstein and the university's Board of Overseers, requesting that an exception to the two-year leave limit for law professors be made for Bell. Michelman would lament after Bell's departure, "Things are in ruins. There is rubble." Bell returned the favor by describing Michelman publicly as having shown great "empathy" for him, his supporters and their cause. Such praise for a white professor, coming from Bell, was both unusual and notable.

Though not a Crit, Michelman made common cause with the far left on a range of issues. A constitutional theorist, he was arguably Harvard's most aggressive champion of liberal judicial activism. Many of his writings were devoted to encouraging greater judicial defiance of self-government. In these writings, he achieved a level of clarity and candor often lacking in the works of other professors and jurists.

Michelman directly tackled the legacy of Justice William Brennan, for whom he clerked on the Supreme Court. He praised the justice tellingly as an "exceptionally gifted doctrinal artificer," a man who rewrote the Constitution at will according to his own "personal vision" and "moral reading." Posing the question "Brennan and democracy—how to have both?" Michelman answered frankly that Brennan had reinvented democracy in a form unrecognizable to the founders of the republic. Brennan's jurisprudence was based on a conception of democracy holding that the people had the right merely "to impress their views upon the Court and the other social authorities, democratically"—that is, to argue their case and beliefs to the courts. Michelman admitted this was not the same thing as traditional democracy: "To press your views upon ruling authorities is not yet to rule."

He dismissed originalism as a philosophical relic impeding social progress. Why, he asked, should modern society follow the intentions of the framers of the Constitution, men of two centuries past whose views are no longer relevant? "Beyond respect and gratitude for their wisdom, what is it that we owe to them?" he asked. Originalists such as Justices Antonin Scalia and Clarence Thomas had argued that only by following the intentions of the framers are judges grounded in something more than their own personal values; Michelman, like almost all Harvard Law professors, rejected such concerns. Michelman also questioned the trend toward direct democracy and public votes. He opined that "representative assemblies or even ... independent judiciaries" had greater precedence in the hierarchy of democratic institutions than initiatives and referenda.

When Professor Field selected someone to chair the five-person subcommittee that would consider drafting a racial harassment code, it made sense for her to turn to Michelman. He was a devout liberal yet not a full-fledged Crit. He was also amicable and courteous in his interpersonal relations. Michelman accepted the responsibility with good cheer, but also with obvious concern about the political balancing act required of him. When asked about whether the subcommittee might draft a speech code, he grew defensive. "I'm virtually a lifelong member of the ACLU," he noted by way of credentials. "I'm a Warren Court baby." He also quickly cited the fact that he had clerked for Justice Brennan two years before the justice authored his opinion in the landmark First Amendment case, *New York Times v. Sullivan.* Like all his fellow liberals on the committee, Michelman would have to weigh this regard for civil liberties against the natural desire to be liked by the African-American students and faculty demanding tough action from the committee.

Another faculty member experiencing this tension was the highly political Christopher Edley. The only African-American professor on the committee, Edley had joined the faculty in 1981, just as Derrick Bell was proclaiming Harvard's deficiencies in hiring minority professors. Edley had previously served in the Carter administration as an advisor on welfare reform. (Some saw the fact that no such reform occurred on his watch as a good indication of his politics.) He worked as national issues director for Michael Dukakis when the Massachusetts governor ran for president in 1988. Edley subsequently took leave from Harvard to return to Washington, this time serving as special counsel to President Clinton. He oversaw the administration's review of federal affirmative action policies—"Mend it, don't end it" was Clinton's ambiguous injunction on the subject—a project which culminated in the president's abortive Race Initiative.

Throughout his career, Edley had functioned like a Democratic political operative as much as a law professor. He was known to be disengaged from class work and tardy in grading papers, perhaps because of his proliferating commitments outside the classroom. His most enduring contribution to American law was cofounding the Harvard Civil Rights Project in 1996. This group, dedicated to generating research, legislation and litigation in support of affirmative action, became a huge cash cow, raking in over $2.5 million a year from high-powered foundations to support a staff of over twenty people—in an operation largely autonomous from the law school. The CRP spearheaded much of the legal work behind the Supreme Court's two landmark rulings in 2003 upholding affirmative action programs at the University of Michigan.

Light on scholarship and academic writings, Edley had one significant literary offering—his book *Not All Black and White: Affirmative Action and American Values.* Here Edley admitted that affirmative action did exact certain social costs from the recipients, in that many whites often questioned whether minorities truly "earned" their accomplishments. But he contended that the benefits of affirmative action, namely economic and social advancement for minorities, far outweighed these costs.

Racial qualifications, rather than "pure personal merit," were an important consideration in awarding professional positions, Edley claimed, because merit and justice are "highly contested matters contingent on characteristics of given situations or organizations, not just on an individual." He branded critics of affirmative action, especially those at the American Enterprise Institute, "racial supremacists" who evidenced a "sociopathic version of white nationalism." When confronting the question of when, if ever, affirmative action should end, Edley's response was vague: " ... When the justification for it no longer exists, when America has achieved racial justice in reality."

In constituting the committee, Dean Clark had at least put together a panel that offered a fair ideological cross-section of the faculty, although it was far to the left of American society itself. The committee members would find themselves buffeted by all the contradictions within modern liberalism. They would be obliged, in particular, to reconcile two conflicting values: unrestricted freedom of expression versus concern that such freedom undermined racial equality. Some liberals desired an open exchange of ideas; others saw this as a prescription for harassment and sought to enact a speech code to shield minorities from what they viewed as inevitable hate speech. This was largely the age-old conflict between liberty and equality itself, a clash noted by Tocqueville and, in more recent years, by Allan Bloom. This friction would frame the debates to follow.

Professor Elizabeth Bartholet captured well the main challenge confronting advocates of a speech code. Though not a member of the committee, Bartholet, a professor of civil rights and constitutional law, had served on the sexual harassment committee in the 1990s and was a widely respected figure at the school. During the Frug-*Revue* controversy, she had been one of the fifteen professors calling for Clark's resignation, and had condemned the "belittling and trivializing" tone of professors such as Dershowitz who had spoken out against the looming threat of censorship. Yet when questioned about the demand for a speech code at Harvard, she said she still had not seen the evidence of "expressed racism" at the school. "I don't see that as a major problem in terms of what's going on, what has gone on, at the law school. . . . I'm just not persuaded there's a problem with general racism."

The white liberals who harbored such skepticism were equally desirous of good relations with pro-speech-code minorities. And so divisions at the law school would continue, as would the specter of censorship as the committee set about its work.

CHAPTER SEVEN

"CONSERVATIVES SHOULD
SHUT UP ABOUT SILENCING"

There was another, forgotten minority at Harvard Law School. This group was not campaigning for a speech code, even though the aggressions against it were actually much greater and more systematic than those suffered by racial minorities at the school. While other minority groups could point to scattered remarks suggesting random prejudice or loutishness, members of this stigmatized group were subjected to concerted abuse virtually every time they expressed their opinions anywhere in the law school. They were conservatives. And now they saw their struggle as part of the intensifying conversation about the limits of free speech.

Prior to the speech-code crisis, conservatives' complaints about the state of civil discourse at the school had been ignored and the legitimacy of their grievances brushed off. Now that the issue of free speech and verbal persecution of minorities had become the major topic of the day, conservatives saw a chance to strike two blows simultaneously. They would work to fight off a speech code while pressing for some sort of official recognition of their own difficulties. As a result of the number and persistence of their complaints, the only minority at Harvard Law that experienced anything approaching genuine persecution would finally earn significant attention from the powers-that-be.

In the fall of 2002, the Committee on Multicultural Unity (one more of the school's multiplying committees with Orwellian titles) surveyed the law school's student body to determine the prevailing attitudes about diversity. One of the most striking results of the canvass was the number of complaints received regarding the intolerance of liberals. Typical was one student's e-mail: "Harvard is horribly liberal, and the orthodoxy is enforced with a vengeance." Another noted, "The greatest problem with diversity at HLS is a lack of ideological diversity."

As the Committee on Healthy Diversity tried to focus on its central professed objective—addressing complaints of race-related intolerance at the school—its members likewise heard numerous claims of discrimination from unexpected quarters. In meetings in November and December, the committee listened as conservative students voiced concerns about heckling and intimidation experienced almost daily at Harvard—in class, Internet chat rooms, and other public or semipublic venues. Professor Martha Field, who said she had not previously heard of this phenomenon, was surprised at the dimensions of the problem, as evidenced by the number of e-mails she received protesting this state of affairs.

Harvard Law School had never been a citadel of conservatism. While charges of leftist intimidation and bias at the school were a relatively recent development, accusations of rampant liberalism were not. Even in the school's first decade of existence, detractors alleged that Harvard was sowing "religious radicalism" by hiring so many Unitarians for its faculty. One history of the law school noted that the influence of Unitarians was a "cause of bitter criticism": "The widespread feeling that

Harvard was a hotbed of religious infidelity or utter atheism may have brought some parents to withdraw their sons or not send them to Harvard in the first place."

By the late 1960s, the student body and the faculty were far to the left of the rest of America. The efforts of Derrick Bell and the Crits in the 1980s further skewed Harvard Law School philosophically and cemented its left-wing reputation. The men and women of the left who gained dominance during this time were not in a sharing frame of mind. An example of this emerging intolerance came in 1987, when the HLS Republicans invited Adolfo Calero to speak at the law school. One of the leaders of the Nicaraguan anticommunist forces, the Contras, Calero was no stranger to combat. Yet the belligerence that awaited him at Harvard was unexpected: a student from Tufts University attending the event rushed the podium before Calero could begin his speech, hurdling a table and throttling the speaker thirty years his senior. After the assailant was pried off Calero's neck and led away, the administration canceled the event, offering the excuse that many liberals had already left and the audience had become ideologically imbalanced. HLS Republicans responded by placing large black-and-white posters on bulletin boards around the school reproducing an Associated Press photo of the attack. Written underneath the photo in large letters was the phrase, "Free Speech at Harvard."

When freedom of speech again became a major issue in 2002, the situation for conservatives had not improved. They routinely experienced both liberal indoctrination in mandatory first-year courses and open, unchecked hostility from other students whenever they voiced a contrarian opinion in class. In the five core courses for 1Ls, students invariably encountered left-tilting lectures and curricula. In Torts, professors frequently taught that even individuals who become injured for lack of common sense—e.g., using a ladder or a lawnmower in an obviously improper way—should be able to sue the corporations that make such products. In Property, much attention was paid to the European conquest of land from American Indians and other peoples around the earth; from this, students were led to conclude that the current distribution of real estate and capital in America is unjust and a legacy of genocide. Students also were instructed that poor people who refuse to pay their rent should be given months of free lodging while courts punctiliously consider their claims.

Contracts classes taught that contracts with lower-income people are often unenforceable. Since poor people suffer from inferior bargaining power when purchasing goods and services from better-off individuals or companies, justice requires that they be able to back out of purchases more or less at will. Civil Procedure, formerly the classic "nuts and bolts" class of law, no longer simply instructed students on the procedural rules of court. Rather, a large portion of class time was devoted to studying "substantive due process." The courts had used this term—which does not appear in the Constitution—as a catch-all theory for judicial activism. (If judges think a law is unjust, they strike it down for violating this court-contrived right to "substantive due process.")

In Criminal Law, offenders were often portrayed as victims whose crimes were caused by social injustice. The death penalty was unjust and should be banned but for one self-help exception: Women who burned abusive husbands in bed, instead of simply leaving them and going to a shelter or a relative's house, were victims of "battered wife syndrome" and should be pardoned. Crimes committed by racial minorities were to be considered, and in some cases excused, in light of cultural misunderstandings.

Students who challenged these notions were often jeered in class. Professors almost never admonished the hectors or interceded in any way. The preferred mode of group intimidation was hissing, which at Harvard Law School had become the sophisticated substitute for booing. Upon completing a remark in class, a conservative student could expect to hear this sibilant objection fill the classroom.

When the Committee on Healthy Diversity began soliciting tales of classroom harassment, seemingly every conservative student who had ever opened his or her mouth in class could recount an incident of mistreatment. Nels Peterson recalled an occasion in his first semester in Civil Procedure. After listening to, by his count, ten students in a row extolling the necessity of judicial activism, Peterson raised his hand and took issue with judges who inject personal philosophy into their rulings. "I think judges should interpret the law, not make it," he concluded.

Rather than a wave of hissing, the response was what Peterson characterized as "loud snickering." Five more students then piled on, repeating the advocacy of judicial activism previously offered. When Peterson raised his hand to respond, he was not called on again (nor was any other student expressing the same view).

Katie Biber, president of the HLS Republicans in 2002, related a similar experience from her second year at the law school. When she enrolled in Professor Heather Gerken's class on election law, Biber recalled, "I was singled out from the beginning as the sole Republican." One of the central issues in class was racial gerrymandering. Biber often found herself the only critic of this practice—even though the Supreme Court has struck down many districts drawn in bizarre shapes for racial reasons. There were days when Biber would gather up her books and tell herself, "I'm never speaking in class again."

Internet chat rooms were another forum for harassment and harsh accusations. Students used these chat rooms to continue discussions online after class adjourned for the day. During one such discussion, a student posted on the Web site his belief that gender is an arbitrary construction of society with no fixed natural basis (a view on which the modern gay-rights agenda is premised). Another student, Jonathan Skrmetti, disagreed and posted a note saying so. "There is a biological difference between men and women that forms the basis of sexual distinctions," he argued. A third student in class, who later became a leader in BLSA, hurled the ultimate aspersion at Skrmetti, accusing him of being a "racist." Skrmetti demanded that the student explain how he arrived at this label. The student answered with this syllogism: Skrmetti's comment was suggestive of Nazism; Nazis were racists; ergo the designation.

FOLLOWING UP ON ITS SURVEY of student attitudes, the Committee on Multicultural Unity sponsored a forum in late 2002 framed with the provocative but, in view of its survey findings, timely question: "Does Harvard Need Conservatives?" Katie Biber, who attended the forum, noted that except for the conservatives there, "Overwhelmingly the response was, 'No.'" One leftist student argued at the forum that the Harvard Law admissions committee should openly discriminate *against* conservatives applying to the school. A quota of conservatives should be enforced, the student argued, because "Harvard is the key to power." One conservative student later observed that if anyone had argued that a quota should be imposed limiting the admission of members of a racial or religious group rather than conservatives, there would be "a tremendous price to pay."

Outside class, there were other attempts to suppress conservative opinions. For many years, conservative student organizations had found it a daunting challenge to keep notices of their meetings and forums posted on public displays. A common way of informing fellow students of upcoming events was to "chalk" classrooms: to write a notice of a future event or meeting at the end of a chalkboard in lecture halls. Often, conservative students returned a day or two after chalking a board to find their notices erased, but liberal messages left intact. An anti-abortion student organization that put up posters on campus billboards with the message, "Smile, Your Mother Chose Life" reported that these were quickly torn down. The same fate befell flyers posted by Students for Protecting America, an ad hoc student group that supported the war in Iraq.

As more conservatives voiced their complaints in the context of the speech-code debate, the issue of ideological discrimination at Harvard Law School finally generated discussion from the school's keepers of liberal opinion. In the spring of 2003, the *Harvard Law Bulletin,* a publication for alumni, devoted a major article to conservatives at Harvard. The student who wrote the article, though a liberal, observed of class discussions: "Rarely will a student hear a professor praise the decisions of Supreme Court Justices Scalia '60, Rehnquist or even O'Connor; right-leaning law and economics scholars like the 7th Circuit's Richard Posner '62 are routinely criticized. It is not unusual in some classes to hear a left-wing student's comments applauded, a conservative's booed." The article noted that after class, conservative students frequently received anonymous, harassing e-mails (which never led to investigations or faculty shakeups).

Even some of the most committed and loquacious conservative students confessed that this sustained repression took a toll. The result was the creation and enforcement of a speech code that was informal but real, one that meant in practice that fewer right-of-center opinions were expressed at the law school. "I think it's a de facto silencing, where you want to choose your battles or get tired of sounding like the 'crazy conservative freak,'" remarked Carrie Campbell, a conservative student leader. Observed another student, Jonathan Skrmetti, "You bring that up [silencing of conservatives] and people either complain about how conservative the law school is— how many students end up going to law firms—or they say the far left is just as underrepresented as the right. And that's just factually wrong."

THE IDEOLOGICAL IMBALANCE began with the faculty. As both tutors and pedagogical traffic cops in the classrooms, professors set the tone for in-class discourse. The shortage of conservatives on the faculty, reflecting decades of bitter dogmatism from Crits and other exclusionary left-wing elements of the school, ensured a lack of intellectual diversity at the school.

This ideological tilt was scarcely unique to Harvard Law School. In the spring of 2003, the *Wall Street Journal* published a national survey that bore out the slant that law students had experienced for decades. The two survey authors noted that even as law schools routinely defended affirmative action in admissions policies as a way of ensuring diversity of viewpoints and life experiences, "These same law schools almost uniformly lack a 'critical mass' of conservatives to offer an alternative to the reigning liberal orthodoxy." The scholars examined the campaign contributions of law professors to determine their political inclinations, poring over all federal campaign contributions of more than $200 by professors at the top twenty-two law schools from 1994 to 2000.

The analysis showed that law professors were both much more politically active and much more liberal than the U.S. population as a whole. Close to one-fourth of law professors had made some sort of federal political contribution, a rate far exceeding that of other citizens. While the American people were split fairly evenly between Republicans and Democrats, 74 percent of professors gave primarily to Democrats; only 16 percent gave to Republicans.

One conservative student contrasted the faculty at Harvard Law with the rest of the nation. Pointing to the 2000 presidential election, he noted, "Half of America is right of center, and only one percent is far left." Yet his hope that "there would be more conservatives" on the law school faculty to remedy this disconnect between Harvard and America had long proved illusory.

Conservative students believed that this imbalance could only impair the quality of education at the school. There were the politically one-sided class lectures and the free rein given to enforcers of liberal dogma against conservative dissenters in class. Professorships at Harvard Law also were positions of power, and as such were a great boon to the left. Tenured professors enjoyed safe positions from which to advocate authoritatively all manner of causes to the rest of the nation. Campus funds also supported left-wing speakers and causes.

As a result, conservative students found they had to be careful about expressing impolitic views in their exams or class papers, while right-of-center professors likewise practiced self-censorship. Students long suspected that grades sometimes reflected professorial bias; how could they not, when many professors considered expression of conservative viewpoints proof of a basic misunderstanding of important issues? One conservative student at Harvard, who intended to pursue a career as a law professor, stated her intention to specialize in some uncontroversial area of law such as intellectual property until she received tenure. Only afterward, she said, would she enter more politically charged niches of law, such as race, gender or bioethics.

Charles Fried believed an institutional bias was at work, one that produced a faculty out of touch with the nation as a whole. "Law schools generally are very lopsided," he observed. "That's too bad, and I do think that in appointments, there's a . . . filter operating" to perpetuate the left-of-center viewpoint.

Dershowitz did not pretend that complaints from conservative students about the liberal political milieu at the school were unjustified. In January 2003, the Diversity Committee invited representatives of the Federalist Society to meet and discuss a possible speech code and the general issue of free speech at Harvard Law. As the discussion roamed to related issues, such as quasi-institutional hostility toward conservative students and the dearth of conservative professors to serve as mentors, Dershowitz replied, "Why should I or other liberal professors go out of our way to help you out? In fact, if we wanted to level the playing field, we would intentionally grade you lower because you get the best clerkships when you graduate"—this because of the alleged abundance of conservative judges.

Still, Dershowitz acknowledged a liberal slant on the faculty and the need for greater intellectual diversity:

The true test for diversity for me is would people on the left vote for a really bright evangelical Christian who was a brilliant and articulate spokesperson for the right to life, the right to own guns ... anti-gay approaches to life, anti-feminist views? Would there be a push to get such a person on the faculty? Now, such a person would really diversify this place. Of course not. I think blacks want more blacks, women want more women, and leftists want more leftists. Everybody thinks diversification comes by getting more of themselves, and that's not true diversity.

A survey of the Harvard Law faculty at the time of the speech-code controversy showed that no such professor existed—and that conservative views were almost never expressed by faculty members. For example, not a single professor advocated originalism, the conservative philosophy of constitutional interpretation holding that judges must interpret the Constitution in light of the intentions of the framers of that document. Throughout American history, this judicial philosophy guided major Supreme Court rulings, with a small number of notable exceptions, until the activism inaugurated by the Warren court. Originalism was the preferred legal philosophy for the nation's leading conservatives, including Justices Antonin Scalia and Clarence Thomas. Yet a survey of the Harvard faculty in 2003 revealed that not one professor advocated it.

When asked to name an originalist, Fried replied candidly, "I can't think of one." He added, "I think such a person would have a hard time getting appointed" to the faculty. In Fried's view, a belief in originalism would make "the whole ensemble of the person" appear out of touch with the law school. Such an applicant would seem like "a Flat Earther in a geography department."

Frank Michelman reiterated this view. An unapologetic proponent of judicial activism, Michelman likewise could not name an originalist on the Harvard Law faculty. But he was quick to add that this exclusion was rational, saying, "It's such a ridiculous doctrine."

The same was true for professors who were anti-abortion or critical of racial preferences in hiring or admissions. The only acknowledged pro-life professor was Mary Ann Glendon, whose writings on family law issues led Pope John Paul II to appoint her to lead the Vatican's delegation to the United Nations' Fourth World Conference on Women in Beijing in 1995. Professor Martha Field contended that there was "a sizable number" of students and faculty who supported abortion restrictions. "There are a lot of pro-lifers" on the faculty, she said. "I bet there are at least eight." Yet the only one she could name was Charles Fried. In fact, Fried supported abortion rights; he was, however, the only professor who openly criticized affirmative action.

"I don't think we're a runaway lefty institution," Field insisted as she commented on the number of complaints about liberal bias she had received from conservative students. "I might like us better if we were, but we're not." This characterization, however, came from a professor who called Dean Clark a "conservative" and clearly had no idea that there were no right-of-center professors on the Harvard Law faculty.

Such an ideological desert, once created, was self-perpetuating. Examples of the sheer intellectual and professional loneliness that is the lot of conservative professors could be found elsewhere in Harvard University. One was Stephan Thernstrom, the Winthrop Professor of History. One of the nation's leading historians (he was a pioneer of the "new social history," which focuses on ordinary people rather than political and cultural leaders) and co-author with his wife, Abigail, of well-received books on race relations in America,

Thernstrom was a political liberal when he joined the Harvard faculty in 1973. As his politics moved toward the center over the years, he found himself the odd man out at dinner parties and faculty social functions. Recalling get-togethers during the 1980s, he said, "When people would be laughing and saying, 'Oh, Reagan, what an idiot,' we [he and his wife] would respond ... and there would usually be some sort of screaming argument. And eventually we would no longer be invited to such parties."

Thernstrom grew even more estranged from the university when he experienced his own free-speech crisis, which arose from one of his courses. In 1988, he and another history professor, Bernard Bailyn, taught a history of ethnic groups entitled "The Peopling of America." Three African-American students accused Thernstrom of being "racially insensitive" for, among other things, reading aloud from the journals of white plantation owners. The students went public with their grievances without even confronting Thernstrom about them first. A university committee investigated the matter, and Thernstrom later complained of the "chilling effect" that such "McCarthyism of the left" exerted on the institution. The silence of university officials in the face of such attacks, combined with other actions that suggested more sympathy for the students than for him, left Thernstrom feeling "like a rape victim." He discontinued teaching the course, saying that race issues are "simply not teachable any more, at least not in an honest, critical way."

Sixteen years later, reflecting on his own career and the state of academic freedom and diversity at Harvard, Thernstrom spoke of the professional ostracism encountered by instructors of the right. "I've basically dealt with it by disengaging," he noted, "I mainly work at home and just go in to teach, which is a change since the 1980s." As for conservatives considering a career as a university professor: "I think untenured faculty who have any conservative leanings would be well advised to keep them a deep, dark secret."

At the law school, such bias not only deprived conservative students of mentors on the faculty, but made it imperative that they seek out lesser-of-two-evil professors for their coursework—those who at least were less partisan than others. Some instructors were simply to be avoided if possible, which limited the range of course selections for right-leaning students. Hard-left professors teaching a mandatory first-year course could not be avoided, and in such cases were to be endured.

Conservative students uniformly found Jon Hanson, a torts professor, especially insufferable. Frequently his lectures included pontifications to the effect that, in the words of one former student, "we should hold a chainsaw manufacturer liable if someone misuses it." His writings bore out this bias. In one law-review article, Hanson argued that the plaintiff's bar was not responsible for the increased filings of tort claims in recent years. He also disputed the notion that the litigation lottery—in which some plaintiffs win $1 million and others $10,000 for substantially similar injuries, depending on the jury and the jurisdiction—is an inefficient way of determining fault and damages. He wrote that "there is ... no great reason to believe that the appropriate balance is not being struck under the current regime," and "there is no reason to place less faith in juries and in tort law than many reformers place in the market." One student recalled that in Hanson's class, conservatives who spoke up were "treated as pariahs."

Another professor known for rough treatment of conservatives was Joseph Singer, who taught property law. Katie Biber remembered that his lectures were "chock-full of insults" to conservatives. The essence of one lecture, she recalled, was "Republicans don't want to pay taxes. They're selfish."

PROFESSORS FIELD, MICHELMAN and others admitted that the avalanche of complaints from conservatives triggered by the speech-code crisis forced a broader discussion of free speech. Yet conservatives, rather than demanding speech codes to protect them from the rough-and-tumble of class discussions, became the main opponents of the proposed speech code. Predictably, the same left that had curtailed conservative speech did not respond to such conservative forbearance in a similarly generous spirit.

Students and professors mostly dismissed conservative grievances. Typical was the response of the student newspaper, the *Record.* A lead editorial in March 2003 took up the allegations that liberal intimidation tactics chilled expression of conservative opinions on campus. The title of the editorial summed up its thesis: "Conservatives Should Shut Up about Silencing."

"What is silencing?" the editors of the paper asked. "Some argue that it is found in the rolling of eyes, the audible sighs when an unpopular view is voiced and classroom responses that treat unpopular opinions as if they should not even have been voiced." Such a view was unwarranted, however—and the solution was for conservatives to grin and bear it. "If a student feels uncomfortable expressing an unpopular opinion, that is largely his own fault and his own choice," the editorial continued. "No one here is incapable of forming a sentence or making an argument. If she stays silent in class because she thinks somebody will boo or hiss, that is her own choice. Given the confrontational profession we are learning, many here would do well [to] start developing thicker skins now."

The paper had treated complaints from BLSA far differently. This disparity was at once striking and indicative of the double standards at the law school. The *Record* had not published a similar editorial after a couple of isolated and boorish racial comments set off a clamor for a full-blown speech code. Yet in the face of decades of coordinated harassment against conservatives in class and out, the recommended course was to take the abuse without complaint.

Not all liberals at the school were as unsympathetic toward conservatives' dilemma. Some liberal professors on the Diversity Committee said they appreciated becoming more aware of the chilling effect on conservative speech at Harvard. Martha Field began a correspondence with one male student in particular who stated that he no longer felt comfortable speaking up in class. "I was impressed by the people who felt if they spoke up, they would be objects of ridicule," Field recalled.

Frank Michelman insisted that he himself had not witnessed incidents such as hissing at conservative opinions in class. But he did acknowledge some difficulty in getting conservatives to speak. "As a teacher, there certainly have been times when I've had to work to get a viewpoint expressed that I thought was out there," he recalled. "I don't doubt these complaints [from conservatives] are sincere." He saw this silencing as the result of a social dynamic whereby students with unpopular views did not want to be regarded as a "leprous outsider." He added that he saw a parallel in the concern about a "silencing effect" for women and minorities. Michelman then added sardonically, "It's interesting that this is coming from those who might not be sympathetic to these other complaints."

Other conservative students noticed greater sensitivity after their complaints had received attention. One recalled a left-wing student commiserating in the only terms the student could understand: "You're just like a minority group." After the article on conservatives at Harvard was published in the *Harvard Law Bulletin* and Katie Biber was quoted regarding the bias that conservatives encountered, Professor Heather Gerken took to e-mailing her after class to thank her for participating.

Ironically, the attempts to silence conservative students often hardened them to the point that they graduated even more set in their views than when they arrived. Nels Peterson, a home-educated conservative from Georgia who described himself as "moderate among Georgia conservatives," said the law-school experience had "tipped the scales" in making him more conservative. Jonathan Skrmetti remarked, "I was a Connecticut Republican. I've been driven a bit rightward in response to" the biased environment.

Peterson added, "I know a lot of it is just reacting to the leftists here. I've gotten to the point that I respect the ACLU" for their generally consistent support of free speech. At Harvard, by contrast, "It's free speech for me and those who agree with me, but not for anyone else."

CHAPTER EIGHT

POETIC INJUSTICE

While the law school was mulling over a possible speech code, another challenge to freedom of speech engulfed the rest of Harvard University. Tom Paulin, the instigator of this controversy, was an Irish-born poet whose verse and public utterances were laced with malice toward Jews. A professor at Oxford University, he had risen to international renown at least as much on the venom of his views as on the quality of his art. In the fall of 2002, Harvard's English Department invited Paulin to read some of his poetry at the Morris Gray Lecture on November 14.

This announcement occasioned little discussion until Rita Goldberg, a professor of literature familiar with Paulin's background and views, alerted other members of the Harvard community to the significance of this invitation. Soon she was firing off e-mails quoting Paulin's observations about Jews who settled on the West Bank: "They should be shot dead. I think they are Nazis, racists. I feel nothing but hatred for them." His poetry exalted and propagated anti-Semitism. In one poem, he referred to the Israeli military as the "Zionist SS" who shot "another little Palestinian boy."

Paulin's depiction of Israel as a "historical obscenity" was seemingly calculated to offend. Just days before the scheduled lecture, the university administration responded to the chorus of concerns. Harvard president Lawrence Summers called the chairman of the English Department, Lawrence Buell, and spoke with him at length about the matter. Buell then announced that Paulin's lecture had been canceled after "it became fully clear to us that Mr. Paulin's visit was likely to produce undue consternation and divisiveness."

While many foes of anti-Semitism cheered this as a blow for civility, others saw the withdrawn invitation as having spread a dark cloud of censorship over the university. If the Harvard administration could bar speakers because of the unpopularity of their views, all manner of other restrictions were equally possible. It fell to one of the most conservative professors at the law school to confront the university's administration over this implicit threat to basic liberties.

When he learned of the Paulin controversy, Charles Fried resolved to defend the paradigm of free speech articulated over the years by so many Harvard Law graduates on the Supreme Court. He believed that professors at the law school were particularly obliged to take up this cause. Rather than dashing off his own letter, he characteristically reached out to other faculty members known for their liberal credentials. The two he turned to—both Jews—would have been uniquely compelling advocates of free speech in this instance. One was Alan Dershowitz, who readily assented. The other was a more careful and more political figure, a professor who had frequently been mentioned as a possible future Supreme Court nominee and who had recently been in the political spotlight as the attorney of record for Vice President Al Gore in the litigation that culminated in *Bush v. Gore*.

Laurence Tribe, like Fried, had a life story that prominently featured flight from religious persecution. Tribe's grandparents left Russia to escape pogroms that were growing in intensity at the turn of the twentieth century. His family entered China, then sailed across the Pacific to San Francisco. Tribe himself went on to Harvard Law School, where he showed himself a brilliant student. After clerking for Justice Potter Stewart (best known for his comment about pornography, "I know it when I see it"), Tribe was invited to join the Harvard faculty. There he received tenure at the age of twenty-eight (equaling Dershowitz's feat) and quickly became one of the law school's intellectual heavyweights.

Much of his legal reputation hinged on a 1,700-page treatise entitled *American Constitutional Law,* first published in 1978. The book became the most frequently cited legal text published in the second half of the twentieth century. Tribe was also commonly sighted in Cambridge, often jogging along the Charles River. Consistent with the informality of the times, he frequently wore running shoes to class along with a crew-neck sweater and slacks. His light blue eyes, which peered out beneath shaggy eyebrows and hair, were among the most legally perceptive in the entire Harvard community.

Tribe achieved public distinction as a leading liberal academic, as well as full-fledged bête noire of American conservatives, in 1987 when he spearheaded the legal academy's opposition to the Senate confirmation of Judge Robert Bork for the Supreme Court. Bork later noted the "protean" nature of Tribe's writings, and indeed his views showed an elasticity of philosophy more suggestive of a politician than a detached legal scholar. It was open to speculation whether this quality reflected Tribe's desire to remain viable as a possible Supreme Court nominee, an aspiration he was commonly assumed to harbor. One conservative legal journal, *Benchmark,* devoted a whole issue to Tribe's legal machinations, with articles entitled "The

Many Faces of Laurence Tribe" and "God Save This Honor-
able Court—and My Place on It." William Bradford Reynolds,
a conservative veteran of the Justice Department under Ronald
Reagan, observed of Tribe, "Every article, every interview,
every speech, even every brief and pleading, seems crafted
with an eye on how the written or uttered word will enhance
[his] chances of becoming Mr. Justice Tribe."

Tribe's commentary on the impeachment of President
Clinton almost a decade later illustrated his deft political touch.
In analyzing whether Clinton's actions in office qualified as
"high crimes and misdemeanors" under Article II, Section IV
of the Constitution, Tribe scrutinized the text of the Constitution and found conveniently that while impeachment might
be warranted for offenses for which Clinton was not charged
(for instance, "Filegate" and "Travelgate"), the offenses for
which Clinton *was* charged—even committing perjury before
a federal grand jury—were not a "defensible basis to impeach
and remove a President from office."

Tribe became something of a Democratic pinch hitter in
the high-profile election cases to come in the following decade.
His greatest national fame arose from his brief service as Al
Gore's lead counsel during the Florida recount following the
2000 presidential election. In a development that must have
been extraordinarily galling for the proud professor, David
Boies replaced Tribe in *Bush v. Gore.* In 2003, Tribe again took
up the Democratic cause in a disputed election, this time the
California gubernatorial recall. Alongside attorneys for the
ACLU, Tribe defended a decision by a three-judge panel of
the Ninth Circuit Court of Appeals to postpone the recall election for six months. The Ninth Circuit, sitting *en banc,* later
unanimously overturned the panel's ruling despite Tribe's zeal-
ous and able argument.

When Charles Fried approached Dershowitz and Tribe about responding to the Paulin controversy, Fried's diplomatic skills—honed by years of surviving at a liberal institution inhospitable to his views—were put to yet another formidable test. There was, for one thing, the fact that Dershowitz and Tribe did not like each other very much. This tension owed to more than simple professional rivalry, although there was plenty of that between Harvard Law's former *wunderkinder.* The two had a history of disagreeing over the proper extent of freedom of speech at Harvard.

The Frug-*Revue* controversy drove a final wedge between Dershowitz and Tribe. True to his normally keen political calculus, Tribe waited until one side in the dispute appeared to be gaining sway over the other. After outrage over the parody had mushroomed, he sided with the left, joining their demands for formal censure of the offending student editors and institutional changes to prevent a recurrence of such an offense. In a speech to the Jewish Law Students Association, Tribe poured out scalding rhetoric, comparing the editors to Holocaust revisionists and members of the Ku Klux Klan (just as Klan members wore white hoods, the authors of the *Revue* remained anonymous to hide their identities). He went so far as to suggest that the offensive material in the *Revue* constituted sufficient evidence to sustain a claim of gender or race discrimination in court. He described these events as a "slow-burning holocaust against women" at the school.

Tribe worked with Crits on the faculty to oust the Clark administration and overhaul the law school in a more left-wing image. He was one of the fifteen professors who signed a letter demanding punishment of the editors and describing the professional climate at Harvard as "misogynist" and "sexist." Apparently concerned that this was not a sufficiently militant gesture, Tribe later confided to Christopher Edley that he was considering resigning from the school in protest *à la* Derrick Bell. Edley praised Tribe and voiced regret that he himself lacked the financial ability to do the same. Tribe ultimately decided against this course and stayed on.

These actions drew the ire of Dershowitz, who worried that free speech was being dumped overboard for the sake of a trendy political cause. In a syndicated column first published on April 22, 1992, Dershowitz deplored the persecution of the *Revue* editors, saying it was creating an "atmosphere of a McCarthyite witch hunt." He pulled no punches in his assessment of the forces of political correctness at work:

> The overreaction to the spoof is a reflection of the power of women and blacks to define the content of what is politically correct and incorrect on college and law school campuses throughout much of the nation.... Women and blacks are entirely free to attack white men (even "dead white men," as they do in describing the current curriculum) in the most offensive terms. Radical feminists can accuse all men of being rapists, and radical African-Americans can accuse all whites of being racists, without fear of discipline or rebuke.

Even though his office was just a few steps down the hall from Dershowitz's, Tribe opted to reply to this polemic in writing, with an interfaculty memorandum. Written the day after publication of Dershowitz's column, the memo depicted his scenario of political correctness as a "crazy mirage." Tribe further trained his fire on Dershowitz specifically, saying, "In the name of courage and iconoclasm, Alan repeats a conventional wisdom that seems to me all convention and little wisdom."

This only further provoked Dershowitz, who responded with his own counter-memo and a running dialogue with Tribe in the press. Some months later, his dander was still up sufficiently for him to offer some pointed words about Tribe in an interview for *Vanity Fair:* "Let's be frank. Larry was one of those who was kicking these students in the balls when they were down, and he should know better." He added, in words reminiscent of Bork's critique of Tribe's machinations, "Larry is going to get a bad case of chapped fingers from wetting them so often and sticking them up to see which way the truth is blowing."

Such tension was the handmaiden of rivalry, and of this Dershowitz and Tribe had no shortage. Both were famous and accomplished men in the nation's most famous law school. Both pulled down huge salaries practicing law outside the law school. (Harvard allowed its professors to practice a certain amount of law as a supplement to their professorial salaries.) At the time of the Frug-*Revue* controversy, Tribe was charging between $775 and $1,200 an hour, a higher rate than that charged by the highest-paid attorneys on Wall Street. Tribe's annual legal income was a staggering $1–3 million. Dershowitz likewise raked in large sums from his high-profile criminal defense work, charging $500 an hour; and he earned more than Tribe when it came to speaking fees and book deals. All this was on top of an ample salary of $140,000 a year at Harvard Law School.

Time had mollified some of the hard feelings between these two before Fried approached Dershowitz and Tribe about the Paulin affair. Dershowitz was an easy sell because of his principled commitment to freedom of expression across the board. Tribe ended up joining the effort as well, possibly because by the political standards of the day, it was much easier to defend free speech for anti-Semites than for speakers insensitive to racial minorities.

The three professors lent their names to a November 15 letter to the editors of the *Harvard Crimson,* the main student newspaper at the university. The short but significant letter from these titans of American constitutional law carried enough heft to set the university abuzz:

> By all accounts this Paulin fellow the English Department invited to lecture here is a despicable example of the anti-Semitic and/or anti-Israel posturing unfortunately quite widespread among European intellectuals. We think he probably should not have been invited. But Harvard has had its share of cranks, monsters, scoundrels and charlatans here and has survived.

Fried et al. then noted the perils of permitting de facto censorship to stand:

> What is truly dangerous is the precedent of withdrawing an invitation because a speaker would cause, in the words of English Department chair Lawrence Buell, "consternation and divisiveness." We are justly proud that our legal system insisted that the American Nazi Party be allowed to march through the heavily Jewish town of Skokie, Illinois. If Paulin had spoken, we are sure we would have found ways to tell him and each other what we think of him. Now he will be able to lurk smugly in his Oxford lair and sneer at America's vaunted traditions of free speech. There are some mistakes which are only made worse by trying to undo them.

The letter contributed to an ensuing national ruckus over the cancellation of the Paulin lecture. Embarrassed, the Harvard administration backed down. The English Department reissued the invitation to Paulin several days later. (A year afterward, Paulin still had not accepted the university's hospitality.)

This victory for advocates of free speech was not without blemish. While the university as a whole had upheld Paulin's right to say abominable things about one minority group, matters were being handled very differently at the law school, where racial minorities had been on the receiving end of offensive speech. An unspoken but clear rule of campus politics had emerged: African-American victims of offensive speech were entitled to greater official protection than Jewish victims. Fried, Dershowitz and Tribe were too polite to note this discrepancy when they penned their letter. Yet the inconsistency was there, and it was obvious.

As for Tribe, he would show no such resolve or interest in the free speech crisis at his own law school. From the outset of the controversy, he completely ducked the issue of a racial harassment code. When this author asked for comment on the proposed speech code at the law school, Tribe replied with various shifting demurrals. He first said, "I am completely overwhelmed with other commitments between now and my argument of an important free speech case in the U.S. Supreme Court on April 23 and will not be in a position to grant any interview on this topic in the interim." When asked after the oral argument, he again avoided the issue. "I'm afraid my schedule has filled up again with a series of pressing academic and family matters, and it doesn't look like I will have the time to respond to your questions until August at the earliest," he stated. "Please forgive me." He never publicly expressed an opinion on the controversy.

In fairness, Tribe's careful reaction was not unusual. Offering a defense of free speech rights for anti-Semites generally did not threaten one's academic career; offering a similar defense for racially offensive people was a different matter entirely.

At least one professor judged Harvard University as a whole to be more intellectually open than the law school—even though the Supreme Court had long looked to the law school for inspiration in securing constitutional liberty. Stephan Thernstrom observed, "I do think the college is a much freer place than Harvard Law School." This was largely a function of the different subset of people attending the latter: "The law school is filled with young, ambitious ideologues and very powerful organized groups. In Harvard College, kids have a million interests," from lacrosse to chess to drama. "In the law school, it seems to me it's a professional place," where students' identities are coterminous with law school and the active organizations are "political, racial and feminist" groups. "I think the law school is probably a very different world. The students are older, more arrogant, better organized." When such organization was being put to the use of constraining freedom of speech, and professors like Laurence Tribe were too distracted or intellectually self-protective to check them, the difference in the atmosphere could only grow more acute.

CHAPTER NINE

THE SOCRATIC METHOD
BECOMES A HATE CRIME

By the time the Committee on Healthy Diversity sponsored its first Diversity Town Hall meeting on November 18, 2002, the administration had changed the committee's name. Gone was the word "Healthy." "There were too many jokes," Dean Rakoff later admitted.

Professor Martha Field opened this first meeting by announcing what she saw as the committee's main objectives. To a crowd of 150 students and faculty, she stated, "We are looking to separate hurtful things from the mainstream of free speech."

When asked about the legality of these possible actions, Field contended that the law school had the right to institute a racial harassment speech code. This was despite the fact that federal courts uniformly had struck down such policies at public universities across the country. She based her analysis on the fact that Harvard is a private institution. "When the government can't do that ... an institution like Harvard Law School can still tell students to respect each other," she insisted. The chairman of the Diversity Committee was giving every indication that a speech code was in the offing.

In response to such provocations, and with members of the media present, Dershowitz was itching for an excuse to unload. In his past dealings with Tribe, Bell and other faculty members, he had shown a decided lack of concern for the niceties of good faculty relations. He would carry the same approach into this meeting, caring little about whose feathers were ruffled when important principles were at stake.

In stirring up such heated interfaculty debate, Dershowitz was carrying on an old Harvard tradition. The fractures in the faculty exposed by the racial harassment flap were hardly new or unique. Disagreements were to be expected among a faculty of ambitious and outspoken lawyers, and throughout its history the law school had not failed to generate significant quarrels over the contentious issues of the day. In the 1920s and 1930s, Professor Felix Frankfurter and Dean Roscoe Pound fought bitterly, hurling at each other claims of anti-Semitism and advocacy of socialism, respectively. Frankfurter had run afoul of Harvard University's president, Abbott Lawrence Lowell, in the 1920s for supporting a clemency petition for two confessed anarchists and convicted murderers, Nicola Sacco and Bartolomeo Vanzetti. (Frankfurter's critics pressed unsuccessfully for his ouster from the school.) Later on, Frankfurter lambasted Dean Pound for accepting an honorary degree from the University of Berlin in 1935, during the heyday of Nazism, and for not supporting three Jewish candidates for teaching positions. Pound lashed out at Frankfurter's support for the New Deal and his attempt, in Pound's judgment, to control the faculty.

Of course, Derrick Bell's efforts to tar the whole institution as racist represented a quantum escalation of such disputes—to the degree that by the time Clark was selected as dean, one Harvard professor anonymously described the law school in the *National Law Journal* as "the Beirut of legal education."

The difficulties of corralling so many strong personalities in such ideologically charged environs would be on display again this night, as talk turned to a muzzling of speech due to the racial affronts of the prior spring. A female African-American student set the tone for the evening when she rose and presented a list of demands from BLSA. The group reiterated its demand for a comprehensive speech code to combat the racism that had recently come to light at the school.

Dershowitz was not going to leave such remarks unchallenged. After the student had finished, he responded, "With all due respect, what you stated is extraordinarily abstract." He demanded that she give an example of offensive language that could be proscribed by a speech code. "Tell me what you want to ban," he said. "I think we have a right to specificity."

The student could cite nothing. As she stammered, she became obviously embarrassed—"flustered," as Dershowitz would later recall.

Such a response was not acceptable, especially given the weighty matters at stake. Dershowitz's reply was caustic: "That's like asking someone to first vote for censorship, and then figure out later what is censored. With all due respect, I find that statement unhelpful."

Randall Kennedy, who had previously avoided the fray, finally decided to end his silence. Having been taunted by Bell as an Uncle Tom, he had kept his head down throughout the speech-code controversy, as he, like his compatriots on the faculty, understood that any public comments tossed into this boiling stew could only give offense to some quarter. He was an affable figure liked by his students, though he was known to come to class poorly prepared at times (one student spoke of him having to stop midlecture and reread the cases to remember their holdings). Despite the abuse he had taken during the

Bell era, he was a mentor and advocate for African-American students and he seemed to cherish this role.

Kennedy had hitherto stayed out of the debate over a speech code even though he had unwittingly given birth to the crisis. It was, after all, in his first-year property class that Kiwi Camara had taken the notes that touched off the firestorm. (That Camara could scrawl such notes while taking instruction from a black professor made his behavior all the more appalling.) Kennedy had not always been such a reluctant warrior. His actions in the world of ideas beyond Harvard showed a certain intellectual courage.

An African-American professor known outside the law school for his popular books, Randall Kennedy wore nicely tailored suits as well as black-rimmed glasses of the style preferred by Derrick Bell, Cornel West and certain other left-of-center intellectuals. There the comparisons ended. As the Diversity Committee convened that evening, Kennedy was putting the finishing touches on a book to be published in the following year that took on the racial left on the explosive subject of interracial adoptions. Kennedy would state flatly in his forthcoming book *Interracial Intimacies* that he "oppose[d] race matching in adoption and foster care, as I object to kindred policies such as 'cultural-competency' screening for adults who seek to adopt or offer foster care interracially. I favor any arrangement designed to place parentless children in the arms of able and caring adults as quickly as possible, without regard to race." He condemned the practice inspired by the racial left of allowing minority children to be adopted only by parents of the same race, calling it "grievously mistaken" and a "destructive practice" that denied parents to hundreds of thousands of children. He noted, moreover, that any such racial discrimination had become "the paradigmatic *disfavored* method of sorting people," and should remain so.

Earlier in 2002, Kennedy had come out with a book that seemed oddly prophetic, and whose relevance was even more compelling given the situation at hand. The title was, in light of recent events, replete with irony: *Nigger: The Strange Career of a Troublesome Word.* Much more than an extended, *Oxford Dictionary*-like history of the title word, the book was rather a starting point for a discussion of the regulation of free speech in regard to race-related language. Noting that "*Nigger* has been belatedly but effectively stigmatized—an important, positive development in American culture," Kennedy saw this progress as calling forth a new set of challenges. "The very conditions that have helped to stigmatize *nigger* have also been conducive to the emergence of certain troubling tendencies. Among these latter are unjustified deception, overeagerness to detect insult, the repression of *good* uses of *nigger,* and the overly harsh punishment of those who use the N-word imprudently or even wrongly."

Kennedy pointed out that the resulting social atmosphere allowed unscrupulous or misguided individuals "to exploit feelings of sympathy, guilt, and anger" occasioned by such racial charges. He cited as an example the Tawana Brawley hoax, in which a young black woman claimed that several white men had kidnapped and raped her and written a racial slur on her body with feces. In Kennedy's judgment, classic works that used the N-word in the process of challenging entrenched racism—most famously Mark Twain's *Huckleberry Finn*—had prompted "achingly poignant" examples of "mistaken protest." He also noted incidents in which a public official in Washington D.C. and a professor at the University of Wisconsin were nearly

ruined professionally by using the same-sounding but etymo-
logically unrelated word "niggardly."

Kennedy took issue with the entire notion of writing up
speech codes in response to such incidents. He related the story
of Keith Dambrot, a white basketball coach at Central Michigan University who clumsily tried to rally his majority-black
team at halftime by saying, "We need to be tougher, harder-
nosed, and play harder.... We need to have more niggers on
the team." Dambrot was insipidly imitating the way his play-
ers talked to each other, and while none of them complained
during or after the speech, university officials told him he would
be fired if he used the term again. When a disgruntled player
who had quit the team subsequently complained about the
matter, the incident snowballed into a crisis that culminated
in the termination of the coach. Kennedy thought the university's original approach—censuring the coach and ordering
him to desist—was "sufficient." University authorities "capit-
ulated too quickly to the formulaic rage of affronted blacks,
the ill-considered sentimentality of well-meaning whites, and
their own crass, bureaucratic opportunism."

The whole theoretical and legal basis for speech codes,
Kennedy argued, was dubious. He directly took on Critical
Race theorists like Charles Lawrence, Mari Matsuda and
Richard Delgado for promoting such measures, saying that
champions of speech codes had "*rightly* lost" in both the courts
and public opinion. "Such proposals," he elaborated, "encroach
upon legal doctrines that have helped to make American culture among the most open and vibrant in the world." Kennedy
explained:

> A list of twenty, fifty, one hundred, or even three hundred racist
> incidents may appear to offer a terrible indictment of race

relations on American campuses—until one recalls that there are hundreds of institutions of higher education across the country. Bearing in mind the numbers of young collegians who are constantly interacting with one another, often in close quarters, is a useful aid for keeping in perspective the catalogue of racist episodes that regulationists point to as the predicate for what they see as urgently needed reform.

Kennedy twisted the knife further by noting the real dynamic at work:

> Proponents of enhanced speech codes portray blacks on predominantly white campuses as being socially isolated and politically weak. Yet the regulationists clearly believe that the authorities to whom they are appealing are likely to side with these students and not with their antagonists.

He concluded by saying that "we may count ourselves fortunate that the anti-hate-speech campaign of the regulationists fizzled and has largely subsided. This particular effort to do away with *nigger*-as-insult and its kindred symbols was simply not worth the various costs that success would have exacted."

Sitting now before the crowd as a member of the Diversity Committee, Kennedy literally faced the choice between supporting a speech code advocated by the strident "regulationists" before him and incurring the vituperation of BLSA and the rest of the campus left. He had witnessed at his own law school—in a chain of events starting in his own class—an overblown series of provocations of the type he had just decried in his book. Surely, if ever there was an example of "overeagerness to detect insult" and "the overly harsh punishment of those who use the N-word imprudently or even wrongly," the backlash against Professors Nesson and Rosenberg fit that description impeccably.

And yet Kennedy would shy away from denouncing the trend toward censorship in fact that he criticized so freely in the realm of thought. This evening, the only opinions he offered were ones designed to ingratiate himself with the speech-code activists. The legacy of Derrick Bell painting him as a racial apostate was surely still on his mind; he did not wish to relive those days. He also had taken heat for his book *Nigger*. Martin Kilson, the first black professor to reach full tenure at Harvard University, lashed out at him with words reminiscent of Bell's. "Here Kennedy has a theory ... that the more freely Whites employ the epithet 'nigger,' the better they'll be able to purge Negrophobia from their souls," Kilson alleged in an utter distortion of Kennedy's argument. Kilson took issue with using a racial slur as the title of the book, which, to Kilson's consternation, had climbed onto the *New York Times* bestseller list. He also alleged that the book would make life harder still for the currently embattled African-American students at Harvard Law School. Consequently, when Kennedy dipped his toe into the scalding waters that evening, his belief that universities should not give in to misguided cries for speech codes was fighting his natural, if less commendable, fear of inviting more abuse from the racial leftists at the school.

Trying to commiserate briefly with the female BLSA representative who had drawn the rough rebuke from Dershowitz, then quickly withdraw from the battlefield, Kennedy spoke up to defend the student. Dershowitz, Kennedy said, was using the same kind of insensitive language that had upset many students the prior spring. "I don't think students should feel embarrassed to have to come back with a response," Kennedy said.

Dershowitz would have none of this. While Kennedy was a professor he esteemed—whom he had, indeed, defended when Derrick Bell tried to marginalize him as a black professor who "thought white"—Dershowitz did not appreciate the grandstanding.

"When they come to ask for a speech code, they should be better prepared," Dershowitz shot back. His next words put Kennedy on ice: "Don't try to silence me, Randy."

Philip Heymann, another committee member, interceded and sought to defuse the situation. Heymann was the first deputy attorney general in the Clinton administration. He resigned after only a year in the position, and declined to offer a public explanation for his departure (it was widely believed that he could not abide the shady ethics then starting to surface at the Department of Justice). He defended Dershowitz by noting that the point he had made was valid. "Making someone uncomfortable should not be prohibited," he stated.

But Dershowitz had provoked a strong reaction from the same powerful forces who had taken down Nesson and Rosenberg. Several members of the audience attacked Dershowitz for insensitivity. One complained that he seemed to think all black students thought alike. Another student recommended that there be mandatory sensitivity training for students.

Dershowitz recalled, "A number of people said I violated the racial harassment code by harassing the student by asking a hard question." But Dershowitz could not be bagged as easily as their other prey. He would survive this confrontation, if with a new reputation at the school for being racially insensitive.

Other speakers buttressed the points that Dershowitz had made. Harvey Silverglate, whom both Dershowitz and Michelman had invited to the town hall meeting, decried the so-called racial harassment policy as a "speech code by another name." True harassment, he noted, would violate existing civil and criminal law. Adding a new code would be just another attempt to outlaw points of view that unsettle people.

Randall Kennedy would make no further public comment on the controversy and would decline to be interviewed about it, although the subject had previously elicited an entire book from him. In December 2002, following this first Diversity Committee meeting, Kennedy traveled to the University of Michigan Law School to deliver a lecture on race-related topics. He stated that the issue of racial reparations (whether the federal government should pay compensation to descendants of slaves) should be studied by a commission—the ultimate political punt.

One student who rose and spoke found himself even lonelier than Dershowitz or Kennedy that evening. In the words of a like-minded student, Jeremy Fielding was the only conservative who "had the guts" to address the forum as a self-described conservative. Fielding used the occasion to point out that there was a group of students who repeatedly faced open harassment for stating their views in class, or for that matter practically anywhere on campus: Harvard Law's conservatives.

As if to prove Fielding's point, as soon as he finished his remarks, the room was filled with hissing—a sign of disapproval from the left-wing students who dominated the forum. Subsequent speakers took pains to deny that such harassment occurred at Harvard Law, even though they had just witnessed a demonstration of it.

THE FIRST DIVERSITY TOWN HALL meeting showed that the drive for a speech code was real and, if anything, had gathered strength since the events of the previous spring. Dershowitz's brief fencing with BLSA's advocate had also exposed just how poorly considered their proposal was. Even as charges of insensitivity rained down on Dershowitz and others who criticized the prospective code, this initial engagement was not without its dividends. It was becoming clear that the reasoning behind the proposed code was shallow and based largely on the emotion of the moment.

Dershowitz summed up the flaw in the argument for a speech code:

> Clearly we were told that BLSA ... was insisting on a racial harassment code parallel to the sexual harassment code. Of course the problem is ... we don't have a *sexist* harassment code. We have a *sexual* harassment code. That is, we prohibit sexual conduct between members of the faculty and students, which is perfectly appropriate. We don't prohibit sexist conduct. I can make a sexist statement and not be subject to discipline. And there's no analogue. There's no "race-ual," there's only racist.

Dean Clark did not attend the town hall meeting. His means of dealing with the controversy that night was to issue a statement through a spokesman. Clark, reporters were informed, would be "very reluctant" to go along with a code. Still, while he was opposed to curbs on free speech, he was keeping all options open until the committee made its final recommendations.

The students and faculty of Harvard Law had come to expect such waffling. Clark had shown that he was not going to jeopardize his reputation or personal relations at the school by taking a firm stance in such a dicey situation. As if to underscore how averse he had become to the ideological conflict inherent in his job, Clark announced, one week after this first town hall meeting, that he was resigning as dean.

"Harvard Law School is a very special institution, and its impact on the world is both great and good," Clark stated in a letter to the law-school community on November 25. "Serving it as Dean has been an indescribably meaningful and varied experience; I feel blessed," added the ex-seminarian. Clark would step down at what he described as an opportune and natural time, as the school was preparing to launch a new fundraising effort.

Clark had come to view the law school in largely material terms, and desired that his record be judged in these terms as well. He would leave boasting that he had secured greater endowments for the school and thereby improved it financially—though higher endowments had been the norm for preceding deans as well. He said he was proud to have hired more professors and improved the student/faculty ratio—specifically, by increasing the number of first-year sections (the former plans for reducing the school's bureaucracy having been fully reversed). Langdell Library had also been refurbished on his watch.

Yet these were very modest accomplishments when measured against the surrender of constitutional principles orchestrated at the same time. His appeasement of the left—first during the Frug-*Revue* controversy, now during the racial harassment crisis—had undermined academic freedom at the school more than any other events in the history of the institution. Students and professors now knew that if they uttered certain politically unpopular ideas or stated them in an abrasive way, they faced sanctions and possible termination of their careers. Later in the month, as alumni learned of Clark's departure, an Associated Press article would run across the country on CNN.com with the headline asking, "Is Harvard Law getting touchy-feely?" The *Wall Street Journal,* armed with materials supplied by Silverglate, likewise published a damaging article about the speech-code crisis. Clark would leave at the very moment when many Americans were hearing disturbing news about the law school and growing concerned about the plight of free speech in Cambridge.

Clark departed from office with something that he seemed to value far more: a heightened reputation among his erstwhile foes. In exchange for accommodating the demands of left-wing students and faculty while dean, he was showered with kind words from leftist professors upon his resignation. No less than Roberto Unger, the *über*-Crit, praised Clark for policies that served to "preserve the openness and multiply the voices" at the law school. Unger also gushed about Clark's "extraordinary stoicism and devotion." Charles Ogletree chimed in as well. The professor whose tenure Clark once had tried to block now said of the outgoing dean, "Bob Clark has the ability to grow and learn.... His growth has been gradual, but I think his acceptance of a whole host of points of view has been rewarding."

Such "growth" had been "rewarding" indeed for the left. Thanks to Clark's inaction and his concern for reputation, the left enjoyed unprecedented dominance at the law school, picking off professors and students who departed too much from orthodoxy. This was the legacy of Robert Clark, a legacy that would have greatly surprised those who touted his elevation to the dean's office more than a decade before.

CHAPTER TEN

WORLDS APART

How had so many Harvard Law students, normally a freedom-loving lot, come to embrace such restrictions on civil liberties? To answer this question it is necessary only to look at the law school culture. The demands pressed by BLSA representatives and allied students at the Diversity Town Hall meeting were well grounded in recent legal scholarship, much of which had fermented right at Harvard. Over the prior decade, these theories had become cutting-edge legal philosophy at law schools across the country, and they provided scholarly justification for speech codes.

The main philosophical case for speech codes came from scholars inspired by events at Harvard Law two decades earlier. The controversy during Dean James Vorenberg's tenure over whether a white professor should be permitted to teach the course "Race, Racism and American Law" had spawned not only protests but also reflection and influential scholarship on the relationship between race and law. Three key scholars would later point to this controversy as the impetus for their seminal works in support of speech codes. Two of these scholars, Charles Lawrence and Richard Delgado, were not professors at Harvard Law but delivered noteworthy guest lectures there while this crisis was unfolding. The other, Mari Matsuda, was then a student at Harvard Law.

These three wrote separate law-review articles proposing, in essence, that the First Amendment be rewritten to accommodate and institutionalize group-identity politics. The threesome, who described themselves as a "motley band of progressive legal scholars of color," agreed with Critical Legal Studies that "areas of law ostensibly designed to advanced the cause of racial equality often benefit powerful whites more than those who are racially oppressed." They sought to change things with writings that advocated creating special rights to protect minorities from disagreeable speech. Like Derrick Bell, Delgado, Lawrence and Matsuda wrote in a personal voice and told of personal experiences. Traditional reasoning and writing, they asserted, were too abstract to allow them to make their points effectively. Delgado defended this approach as necessary for tearing down legal custom: "Stories, parables, chronicles, and narratives are powerful means for destroying mindset—the bundle of presuppositions, received wisdoms, and shared understandings against a background of which legal and political discourse takes place."

Delgado fired the first major shot in the philosophical war for speech codes. In 1982, the *Harvard Civil Rights–Civil Liberties Law Review* published Delgado's article, "Words That Wound: A Tort Action for Racial Insults, Epithets and Name-Calling," which advocated creation of a tort action for racial hate speech. Delgado drew an analogy to the psychological and other harms suffered by victims of libel and slander, arguing that if the latter could be actionable torts, so could hate speech, for both "torts" caused similar injuries. Lawrence and Matsuda would add to this framework, with Matsuda specifically making the case for speech codes in institutional settings to address face-to-face, one-on-one insults based on race or sex.

This new line of thought resurrected language from old Supreme Court rulings once spurned by liberals. The 1942 Supreme Court case *Chaplinsky v. New Hampshire* became raw material for coining this new proposed tort. *Chaplinsky* gave the nation the "fighting words" doctrine, which held that the government could ban words that "by their very utterance inflict injury or tend to incite an immediate breach of the peace." Decades later, the Supreme Court overturned this language, upholding restrictions on free speech only in those instances when speech is "directed to inciting or producing imminent lawless action and is likely to incite or produce such action." The Supreme Court in later years would hold that states could not ban even such things as burning crosses in public except in very restricted circumstances.

The labors of Delgado, Lawrence and Matsuda provided philosophical encouragement for the campaigns that soon heated up across the country to codify restrictions on speech at colleges and universities. During a five-year period in the 1990s, more than two hundred such institutions adopted anti-hate-crime regulations for students or faculty. The University of Michigan prohibited expression that "creates an intimidating, hostile, or demeaning environment for educational pursuits, employment or participation in University sponsored extra-curricular activities." A federal district court later struck down these restrictions as unconstitutional, as did a federal court reviewing a similar speech code at the University of Wisconsin. In the Michigan case, the court overturned the code because it barred language well beyond the "fighting words" ban upheld in *Chaplinsky*. In the Wisconsin case, the court rejected the Delgado-derived analysis by declaring the language from *Chaplinsky* "defunct." The court noted also that the Wisconsin speech code was not content-neutral because it singled out racist speech.

By the time Harvard Law became embroiled in its own speech-code crisis, supporters of such a code were promoting a policy contrary to settled law. The fact that they were working against the legal grain did not discourage BLSA members or other students in the pro-code camp. They realized that they were pressing theories in vogue in legal academia but not yet in the judiciary. Knowledgeable observers like Harvey Silverglate could only look on these developments in amazement. "I don't think they assign First Amendment cases at Harvard Law School anymore," he remarked. "They study civil rights but not civil liberties."

The popularity of race-and-the-law theorizing bespoke a broader social problem at Harvard Law, as indeed throughout American higher education. The balkanization of the student body, a hard fact of life since the 1960s, became even more salient in the debate over a racial harassment code. Many white liberal students, while striving to appear sensitive to the issues raised by African-Americans, were reluctant to see a speech code imposed on the school. The proponents of such a code were almost entirely, and visibly, African-American. This divide was emblematic of the racial disunity and self-segregation that had characterized student life at Harvard for over thirty years.

From meals at Harkness Commons to study groups in Langdell Library to e-mail lists and chat rooms, black students by and large preferred to associate with one another exclusively. The divisiveness once urged by the Black Panthers had congealed into student life at Harvard, and respectable defenses of separatism had been penned by the likes of Derrick Bell and Cornel West. Fifteen years before, Allan Bloom had lamented of American higher education that "the substantial human contact, indifferent to race, soul to soul, that prevails in all other aspects of student life simply does not usually exist between the two races." The existence and fervor of calls for a speech code at Harvard underscored this point as few other events could.

A poll of students taken university-wide in April 2003 revealed the extent of this fragmentation. The *Crimson* asked Harvard University students, "To what extent do you think ethnic/racial groups at Harvard self-segregate, on a scale of 1 to 5, with 1 being not at all and 5 being a great deal?" More than 50 percent of respondents chose 4 or 5.

Leaders of black student associations saw nothing wrong with this. The president of the Association of Black Harvard Women stated that "self-segregation" would be better termed "self-empowerment." Harrel E. Conner, former brotherhood chairman of the Black Men's Forum, even took issue with the proper scope of the term "community." When he refers to the Harvard community, he explained, he meant only black students. "The community ends at the black community," he said.

BLSA's extremism was consistent with this outlook. Professor Ogletree's notion that the black community held a conception of free speech different from the rest of American society—a view that allowed for restrictions on free speech to curb racism—held sway over the BLSA members who looked to him and other race theorists for guidance. If there was no broader community to be concerned about, as they believed, why not treat this alleged African-American view of free speech as absolute?

These developments troubled many white students at the law school, but none more than the small group of self-described conservatives. More than anybody else at Harvard

Law, they had encountered limits on free speech, for they had endured the catcalls and casual discrimination that were their daily experience at the school. They recognized that there were normal and necessary limits on speech in the classroom—for example, students might speak only if called on, and could be cut off when they spoke for too long or wandered into irrelevant subjects. But they understood better than most that latent in the campaign for a speech code was the quest for ideological censorship. Moreover, the forces championing these changes were left-wing students who were notoriously intolerant toward those of *any* color who disagreed with them.

The university's disinvitation of Tom Paulin and a recent act of official censorship at the business school reinforced these fears at the law school. In November 2002, the editor of the *Harbus,* the weekly student newspaper of the Harvard Business School, quit after the business school administration warned him not to publish a cartoon parodying the ineffectiveness of the CareerLink Web site at the school. The cartoon, drawn by a student at the business school, depicted a computer logged on to "HBS CareerDink" with numerous pop-up announcements filling the screen, including one saying "incompetent morons." The MBA program director called the editor into his office to deliver a "verbal warning," the first step in the disciplinary process. The editor subsequently resigned. Though many recognized this censorship to be an administrative abuse of power rather than an ideological act, still it was yet one more example at the university of how easy and tempting it would be for the guardians of a speech code to use the device to silence their critics.

Law students, particularly conservatives, organized in opposition to these trends. A 2L (a second-year student) named Nels Peterson led this effort. As a 1L, he had witnessed in his torts class the exchange that swept Professor Rosenberg into the speech-code controversy. Peterson started a group called Students for Free Speech. It grew to about forty official members in the student body—a respectable number given the paucity of conservatives and libertarians at the school. SFS monitored developments regarding the speech code and sent out e-mail updates to members and supporters. The group also worked with Harvey Silverglate's organization, the Foundation for Individual Rights in Education (FIRE), to keep the public informed of recent developments.

For all their profound differences, one thing that both left and right could agree on was the need to shun and socially punish Kiwi Camara and Matthias Scholl. As the administration still pondered whether greater official penalties could be meted out to the two offenders, one student mustered enough sympathy for them to summarize what had already befallen them in a letter to the *Record:* "The two students responsible for the racist incidents of last spring have already suffered public obloquy, ostracization [*sic*], discipline from the administration, withdrawn job offers, and may have had their legal careers ruined. A regime that visits even more punishment upon others like them verges on cruelty."

In the end, there was little the school could do to formally penalize Camara and Scholl. The administration issued a rebuke to Scholl for violating school policy in sending out an anonymous e-mail. Given that the Supreme Court had recently upheld a constitutional right to anonymous speech under the First Amendment, even this mild sanction would have been unlawful if issued by a public university. Camara was not punished.

Such official actions were overkill in any event. The informal shunning that the two earned was severe enough. By way of defending the status quo at the law school *sans* speech code, Nels Peterson noted, "Kiwi and Matthias are not having fun at this place. The Holmesian marketplace is alive and well."

The two students had never fit in. Even conservative students, when asked to describe Camara and Scholl, uniformly described them as "marginal guys," "outcastes" and "outliers." Scholl at least enjoyed a preexisting relationship with a Boston firm before the scandal hit, which meant that his professional prospects, though restricted, were not obliterated. This was not so for Camara. A young man six thousand miles from home, barely of adult age, he soon found himself without a friend at the school.

"I just thought Kiwi's an idiot," recalled Jonathan Skrmetti about learning of Camara's posted notes. It was immediately obvious to him and to the rest of the student body what Camara had done: "He's just sort of destroyed any future he had." The extent of this self-destruction became evident soon after the story of Harvard's racial troubles broke in the national media. First came the threatening e-mails. Camara was forced to change his e-mail address after receiving death threats. One author threatened to beat him "to a bloody pulp" in Harvard Yard; since he lived in a dormitory close to Harvard Yard, Camara took the threat seriously. He forwarded this e-mail and the others to Harvard University police, who failed to identify the authors.

Even conservative and libertarian student organizations, filled with members supposedly resistant to calls for censorship, pressured Camara to resign from their mastheads and rosters. "I tend to come out on the conservative side of things," Camara said of his politics, describing himself as a "classic liberal." Upon arriving at Harvard, he had promptly joined what he called the "conservative trinity" of organizations: HLS Republicans, the Federalist Society, and the *Harvard Journal of Law and Public Policy* (JLPP). All three ultimately asked him to sever his ties with their organizations. The editor in chief of JLPP personally requested that Camara resign as an editor. "They didn't want the negative publicity," Camara said.

One of the few student organizations at Harvard that did not expel Camara was a ballroom dancing group. When the members feared he would run for president, they scrambled to round up another student to run in order to prevent him from being elected. The students involved in this maneuver were unapologetic. "Kiwi is radioactive," one said flatly.

He had come to Harvard Law School with the goal of becoming a well-paid corporate lawyer, the typical aspiration of students there. These dreams were now gone. He had clerked at a large law firm in Los Angeles the summer right after the scandal erupted; at that time, the firm could not revoke its offer without potentially making unwelcome news itself. The following year, firms showed no such restraint.

"There were a few offers that I lost," Camara acknowledged. One prominent New York firm gave him a "fly-out," an all-expenses-paid trip so that the firm's partners could interview the potential recruit. After the firm "wined and dined" him, no offer came—a very rare occurrence for a Harvard 2L. At another firm, Camara met with the hiring partner and openly shared what had happened the previous spring. This firm offered Camara a summer position, then later rescinded it (apparently the hiring partner had failed to share the information with the rest of the firm). Another partner from the firm told Camara of this revocation after hosting a dinner in Cambridge for the firm's potential summer clerks. The partner called Camara two hours after the event—evidently after learning of Camara's notoriety from other students—to tell him the firm's "full partnership" had revoked their offer.

Camara lost all opportunities for a law-firm clerkship for the summer after his second year, the crucial summer during which law students line up full-time employment for after graduation. He ended up teaching a political science course that summer at his alma mater, Hawaii Pacific. His plans to practice corporate law at a Wall Street firm dashed, Camara prepared to pursue a career in academia. Professor Charles Nesson offered to write him a recommendation.

Camara and Scholl avoided the media as much as possible. Other than speaking to the *Record,* neither granted an interview. But the media found them, and calls and e-mails rolled in from the *New York Times* and CNN. (The *Times* article later inaccurately described Camara as Caucasian.) The most tenacious suitor, Camara recalled, was Jeffrey Toobin, then writing an article for the *New Yorker.*

Asked if he had regrets, Camara said he had one: "I would not have posted the outlines." For this horrendous juvenile mistake, in which he managed to offend the entire Harvard Law School establishment, Camara would pay dearly. Rarely if ever had a young man experienced a lonelier walk through higher education.

CHAPTER ELEVEN

UN-MARTIAL LAW

Other events external to Harvard Law accentuated how far it had moved from the political mainstream of the nation. As the law school considered a speech code, America prepared for war. While the American people overwhelmingly supported both the military and the war effort at its outset, most students at Harvard and its law school did not.

The attacks on the World Trade Center and the Pentagon stunned and transfixed the law school as they had the rest of the nation. The law school administration soon realized that conducting classes that day was futile; after the north tower of the World Trade Center collapsed, Dean Clark canceled classes for the remainder of the day. Many students then huddled around the two large televisions in Harkness Commons, watching the news reports and images of destruction in silence.

The next day, most professors conceded the obvious and devoted much of their class time to discussing the atrocities. The thrust of the conversation was very different from what could be heard in offices and restaurants and homes throughout the nation. The discussion was, in the words of one student, "basically a you-had-it-coming session." Only the fact that a large number of students were from New York or had relatives or friends killed the day before tempered the outpouring of

169

anti-Americanism. One student remarked, "Virtually every international student said, 'America had it coming.' But there were a lot of American students who said the same thing."

This reaction spilled over into the student newspaper. Letters to the editor of the *Record* argued that America was responsible for the attacks. Two columnists in the *Record,* purportedly offering "both" sides of the debate over why the attacks happened, instead demonstrated that at Harvard, "both" sides meant "left" and "far left." One writer decried America's "global corporate capitalism" for stirring up foreign animosity. The other blamed, among other examples of American imperialism, U.S. support of Israel. He argued that "our continued support for Israel's colonization of its Palestinian frontiers probably doesn't impress your average Palestinian or his supporters in other countries." Another student wrote it was a "certainty that a U.S. invasion of Afghanistan will produce significant human rights violations." In a well-publicized forum after September 11, Professor Frank Vogel, director of the Islamic Legal Studies Program, condemned in advance any military action against Muslim countries. He proposed instead that Osama bin Laden, the mastermind of the attacks, be tried in an Islamic court.

As war clouds gathered in the following months, the law school and the rest of the university set itself even more firmly against the mood of the nation. While the rest of the country supported the military as it prepared for operations in the Persian Gulf, the law school became the site of greater hostility than the school had experienced since the 1960s. Ironically, even more than the outbreak of war, the source of this ill will was the military's "don't ask, don't tell" policy barring open homosexuals from serving in the ranks. Harvard had banned military recruiters from interviewing students on campus in the 1960s as a protest of the Vietnam War. In 1979, the law school had instituted this ban as an expression of "anti-discrimination" policy against the military's ban on open homosexuals serving in the armed forces. This policy was perpetuated through the 1990s as a response to the modified "don't ask, don't tell" policy of the military.

Matters came to a head in May 2002, when the Air Force sent a letter to Dean Clark claiming that the school's policy of forbidding military recruiters from interviewing there violated federal law. The Solomon Amendment, passed by Congress in 1996, prohibited the federal government from dispersing research funding to universities that failed to give military recruiters the same access to campus interviews that other companies and employers enjoyed. At stake was $328 million in federal funds that might be denied to the university if the law school did not give the military the same access as other recruiters.

The dispute meant little as a practical matter. Few Harvard Law graduates would forgo corporate professional opportunities for a career in the armed services, especially after incurring a large student debt to obtain their degree. Still, this ban represented yet another limitation on free speech at the law school. All manner of corporate recruiters could come to Harvard Law to interview students, but the U.S. military was forced to interview interested students off-campus.

As the military pressed the issue, Dean Clark characteristically began to buckle—and to shift the blame. In late August 2002, after first conferring with the gay-rights student organization Lambda, Clark decided to lift the ban on military recruiters. He then released a letter explaining his decision. The bottom line was the bottom line: Harvard could not afford to lose its federal funding. Yet, "To say that this decision is just

about money trivializes the significance these funds have on
... scientific research that can lead to cures to life-threatening
illnesses and debilitating diseases," the dean maintained. He
blamed federal and military officials for coercing the law school
to come into compliance with the Solomon Amendment. In
an e-mail to students, Clark insisted, "Our decision to permit
military recruiters access to the facilities and services of OCS
[Office of Career Services] does not reduce the Law School's
commitment to the goal of nondiscrimination on the basis of
sexual orientation."

As the Cambridge community watched the spectacle of
a law-school dean complaining about having to follow federal
law, the campus left erupted over this revision of policy. Gay-
rights supporters were overwhelmingly in the majority at Harvard, and indeed the homosexual community had become a
sizable minority on campus (some estimated they constituted
10 percent of the student population). The announcement that
military recruiters soon would be coming to Harvard offered
a "Stonewall" moment for campus gay-rights advocates.

A protest rally was planned and announced, with adver-
tisements placed throughout the law school. These included
plastic toy soldiers painted pink and placed atop desks throughout the school's classrooms. Gay-rights activists signed up for
military interviews just to block out the time slots. Interview-
ers dealt with the subterfuge by adding extra slots.

On October 7, 2002, hundreds of students, faculty and
administrators rallied against the "don't ask, don't tell" policy
in front of Langdell Hall. They carried aloft signs bearing such
slogans as, "Dick Cheney: Let your daughter serve!" (a reference to the fact that one of the vice president's daughters was
a lesbian). The rhetoric of speakers was spirited but uninspired
by Harvard standards; the best that Professor Heather Gerken

could do was quote the title of a recent book by Democratic political operative James Carville: "We're right and they're wrong." Gerken went on to accuse the Bush administration of using the terrorism of September 11 as a pretext to enforce the Solomon Amendment, thereby pandering to "right-wing" Republican elements.

Dershowitz took a turn at the podium as well. "This is simple extortion," he exclaimed, denouncing the Solomon Amendment and the law school's capitulation to it. He urged the school to challenge the legality of the policy, and in subsequent weeks he began preparing in earnest for possible litigation. He seemed oblivious to the fact that the school's ban on military recruiters was an act of censorship of the type that he normally inveighed against.

Janet Halley, another law professor, received an enthusiastic response. With a stocky frame, masculine demeanor and silver-streaked, close-cropped hair not unlike that of the military recruiters at issue, Halley had emerged as one of legal academia's leading advocates of "queer theory," or the project of writing the gay-rights agenda into the nation's laws. Her writings wove together theory and practice as she sought to lay a philosophical foundation for same-sex marriage and other aspects of the revolution she advocated, and to chart the politically smartest course toward those objectives.

Noting that "remarkable changes in identity politics over the past decade, most notably the emergence of queer identity and of an unrepentant movement of self-described bisexuals, have complicated gay and lesbian communities," Halley attempted in one law-review article to deal with the nature-versus-nurture argument over the origins of homosexuality. "Many gay men, lesbians, bisexuals, and queers reject the view that they constitute a minority distinguished by a stable, natural identity," she observed at the outset as she questioned the natural, genetic basis of sexual orientation. Ultimately, Halley threw up her hands and skirted the central issue of whether homosexuality is a product of nature or of environment and choice. She stated instead that "pro-gay legal argument should not focus on positive claims of biological causation, or on pure constructivist claims that homosexuality is a historically contingent artifact, but should repair to a common middle ground." That would mean adopting "legal strategies that emphasize the political dynamics that inevitably attend sexual orientation identity—no matter how it is caused.... Litigating on common ground is thus not only the right thing to do—it is also more likely to work."

Halley was also one of the architects of *Lawrence v. Texas,* in which the U.S. Supreme Court overturned a Texas law against sodomy as violating the Constitution. In her article "Reasoning about Sodomy: Act and Identity in and after *Bowers v. Hardwick,*" Halley noted that homosexuals needed to stress for pragmatic reasons that heterosexuals also can run afoul of sodomy statutes. "We can form new alliances along the register of acts," she wrote, sounding much more like a political strategist than a detached legal scholar. "From that vantage point the instability of heterosexual identity can be exploited, and indeed, undermined from within." Distinct echoes of this reasoning could be heard in the Supreme Court's analysis in *Lawrence,* handed down in 2003 (which stressed that sodomy laws historically have dealt with "nonprocreative sexual activity more generally" rather than just homosexual relations).

While a vociferous advocate of expansion of existing freedoms for homosexuals, Halley was more ambivalent about freedom of speech, particularly at Harvard. She emerged as one of the school's leading critics of the Solomon Amendment, and urged the law school to continue its prior policy, which barred military recruiters from speaking to Harvard Law students on campus. When asked how she would square a liberal commitment to free speech with her opposition to military recruitment on campus, Halley replied, "I don't see how that's a free-speech issue. This is a private institution." (When this author noted that by banning military recruiters, Harvard was restricting the flow of information regarding employment opportunities to its students, she abruptly terminated the interview by hanging up the telephone.)

At the rally, Halley challenged the "don't ask, don't tell" policy as not only anti-gay but anti-sex. The policy, she explained, irrationally discouraged certain sexual behaviors and attitudes. Halley also gloated about the prevalence of homosexuals at the school. "If I came to Harvard Law School and I had to enforce 'don't ask, don't tell,' I would have to discriminate against almost everybody," she told the crowd exultantly. "Your homoeroticism is built in, and believe me, I have seen it," she added, to lusty cheers.

Not to be outdone, and with his legacy at stake, Dean Clark also addressed the rally. He explained why the law school had submitted to federal authorities, even though the "don't ask, don't tell" policy was "horrible." To underscore this posture, henceforth every e-mail sent out by the administration to members of the law school community that discussed military interviews carried a disclaimer about the law school's disagreement with the policy.

THE UNREST OVER "don't ask, don't tell"—a policy adopted by the Clinton administration—was barely subsiding by the time war came to Iraq. The left continued its posture of disdain toward the military and its mission. Twelve years earlier, when the HLS Republicans attempted to celebrate the victory in the Gulf War, campus protesters tore down and defaced flyers announcing the event. Now, with a different George Bush as president, the prospect of war sparked an even more visceral reaction.

At 12:30 P.M. on March 20, 2003, a student walkout disrupted classes throughout the university. Over a thousand students walked over to gather on Harvard Yard in protest—the second-largest crowd in the history of the university, according to the *Harvard Crimson.* One university professor, Brian Palmer, told the press that the war was merely a cynical ploy to help Bush get re-elected. "Military war is a cover for class war," he said. The protesters appeared to be a collection of young students enjoying the afternoon off and graying, unbowed ex-hippies reliving their glory days.

The crowd was large because it faithfully represented the dominant view at Harvard. The *Crimson* conducted a survey of four hundred Harvard students at the outbreak of the war, and found that 56 percent opposed the war. They were equally divided between "strong" and "somewhat strong" degrees of opposition. Of the 34 percent who supported military action, most did so only "somewhat." By contrast, a Gallup poll conducted the same day found that three-quarters of the American people supported the decision to go to war.

Although no poll was taken of students at the law school, there was scant evidence that they were any more supportive of the war. Peace flyers denouncing the war appeared throughout the law school, while pro-war flyers were quickly torn down.

As usual, the administration set the tone best of all, announcing that the law school would provide counseling for students who might be feeling high levels of stress or anxiety over the conflict. As young men and women of the same age cohort were offering their lives in defense of the national interest, the administration of Harvard Law School offered only therapy.

CHAPTER TWELVE

BREAKING THE CODE

A year after the rally of April 15, 2002, the movement for a speech code at Harvard was clearly faltering. Kiwi Camara, Matthias Scholl, Charles Nesson and David Rosenberg had already drawn tough punishment: social ostracism and evaporated job prospects for the students, humiliation and spoiled careers for the professors. Also, tempers had cooled over the year that had elapsed. Skepticism from national media elites, including some normally reliable liberals alarmed by the prospect of a speech code, had challenged the rationale for this proposal. A year after the provocations and the resulting rally, not a single Harvard Law professor—not even Charles Ogletree or Christoper Edley—had publicly endorsed a speech code.

The Diversity Committee continued with its work amid these shifting currents. As the Michelman subcommittee considered its options, four main possibilities emerged. The first was, in Martha Field's words, "to do nothing." Second, the committee might outline ideals and aspirations for student and faculty conduct, but without authorizing sanctions for violations. Third, the committee might recommend regulations prohibiting harassment or intimidation—a modified speech code. In order to penalize a violator of these rules, the school would

179

have to find specific intent to harass or intimidate; there would be no sanctions for speech alone. Fourth, the code might proscribe outright certain "hateful speech."

Field described the fourth option as "an educational experience" which, by her account, served mainly to show the "pitfalls" of such a speech code. She stressed in the spring of 2003 that this option was not a "real possibility." One student on the committee had floated the idea, but quickly acknowledged how impractical it was (after some questioning and probing in a manner less confrontational than Dershowitz's methods at the first town hall). That the professor chairing the committee now was publicly dismissing a "speech-only" racial harassment code—after she and the administration had once treated the idea as a distinct possibility—showed how far the ground had shifted.

Frank Michelman, for his part, tried to hitch his wagon to the First Amendment. In April, the U.S. Supreme Court handed down its decision in *Virginia v. Black,* an important First Amendment case. The Court held that a state could constitutionally ban cross burning that was "carried out with the intent to intimidate," partially reversing its ruling on the same issue a little over a decade before. The day after the opinion was handed down, Michelman pointed to *Black* as the lodestar for any potential speech code at Harvard Law School. He noted, however, that the speech/conduct at issue in the case— burning a cross—was unlikely to replicate itself at Harvard. "How much conduct that has much chance of occurring here would [a *Black*-inspired speech code] catch?" he asked rhetorically.

"Any rule proposed for this place must conform to basic First Amendment principles," Michelman insisted as his subcommittee met in the spring. He cited the Massachusetts Civil

Rights Act as "probably" requiring this. The MCRA applied to private as well as public institutions, he noted, and existing First Amendment law would not allow a wide-ranging speech code.

Here his reasoning was circular. As Harvey Silverglate acknowledged, recent U.S. Supreme Court rulings had upheld the right of private institutions under the First Amendment to do things that public institutions could not. Since Harvard was a private university, if it adopted a speech code that conflicted with the Massachusetts law, the federal courts might well overturn the state statute as violating the First Amendment—not the right of free speech, but a second, court-invented right: the right to private "association." Substantial case law had developed recognizing this new First Amendment right, and these rulings might have allowed Harvard to adopt a speech code. As Dershowitz showed in the JAG (judge advocate general) military recruitment controversy, another dispute involving associational rights, there were plenty of experienced lawyers on hand ready to litigate the matter.

Supporters of a speech code and expansion of affirmative action kept the heat on as best they could. In early March, Lawrence Summers, the newly appointed president of Harvard University, hosted a town hall forum at the law school. When Summers arrived that evening to speak, protesters stood outside in the cold evening air on the steps leading up to Austin Hall, to deliver a message of sufficient intensity to permeate the president's gruff exterior. An umbrella group calling for "Diversity in Education: Action Now!" (DEAN) had collected over 250 signatures demanding a new dean even more receptive to affirmative action than Clark had been. Also presented was a demand for a permanent Hispanic member of the faculty. The call for an American Indian professor seemed inevitable as well: The previous month, the law school had established a chair for the teaching of Indian law, funded by the Oneida Indian Nation in central New York (with gambling proceeds from the tribe's casino).

Despite these and other protests, the "Difficult Conversations" workshops—once a proud sign of putative progress at Harvard—were sputtering. A voluntary workshop held the day after Summers' talk showed that when attendance was no longer mandatory, people voted with their feet. Only sixteen people showed up. One observer estimated that the number of Harvard Law students present was in the single digits. This student wrote to the *Record* to complain about the odd juxtaposition of events. The low turnout for the workshop following the well-attended protest the night before, the writer observed, "indicates strongly that Harvard Law students would much rather clamor about supposed administration inattention rather than acknowledge and participate in constructive activities the school has instituted to address the very topics in which students claim to have a significant interest."

As another summer came and dispersed the law school's members to their various professional pursuits, a letter arrived from the U.S. Department of Education to underscore the high stakes in the speech-code dispute. In July 2003, Gerald Reynolds, head of the department's Office for Civil Rights, mailed letters to Harvard and other colleges and universities reminding them of the "central importance" of freedom of speech on campus and the First Amendment. Prompting Reynolds' letter was the specious argument being made by campus administrations across the country that federal regulations required speech codes.

Reynolds clarified that his office enforced civil rights regulations that were "intended to protect students from invidious discrimination, not to regulate the content of speech." Specifically, he disputed the notion that harassment should be defined as including "all offensive speech regarding sex, disability [or] race"; rather, there must be conduct so "severe, persistent or pervasive" as to impair the student's ability to learn. He noted that a private institution that imposes such limits is not required to, but does so "on its own accord." It remained to be seen if Harvard would "plead the First" (saying the First Amendment prohibited such a code) or if speech-code proponents would call their bluff.

MANY HOT POTATOES awaited Dean Clark's successor; but the new dean would at least allay one diversity concern. On April 3, 2003, President Summers announced the appointment of Professor Elena Kagan as the first female dean in the history of Harvard Law School.

Kagan had taken the traditional route to a Harvard professorship. After obtaining degrees from Princeton and Oxford, she had graduated *magna cum laude* from Harvard Law in 1986. She clerked for Judge Abner Mikva on the U.S. Court of Appeals for the D.C. Circuit, then for Justice Thurgood Marshall on the Supreme Court. Both Mikva and Marshall were arguably the most liberal judges on their respective courts; Mikva would later become a fixture in the Clinton administration, and the hands-off Marshall was well known for allowing his clerks to write up ultraliberal court opinions. After working for a corporate law firm in Washington, Kagan joined the faculty of the University of Chicago Law School. She later took leave to work in the Clinton administration—first as associate counsel to the president, then as deputy assistant to the president for domestic policy and deputy director of the domestic policy council.

Normally such public service would have been a sterling credential in a formidable professional resumé. But Kagan had worked at Clinton's right hand during an especially controversial time in a rocky presidency. She was counsel to the president when Filegate, Travelgate and a succession of scandals involving official abuse of power were cascading down on the administration (Clinton also began his relationship with Monica Lewinsky during this time). Unlike her comrade on the Harvard faculty, Phil Heymann, she had not quietly left the administration after a brief period of time—apparently just long enough, in Heymann's case, to take the measure of the administration's ethics. Instead, Kagan remained at Clinton's side throughout his subsequent impeachment.

In June 1999, Clinton nominated Kagan to the D.C. Circuit Court of Appeals. Given her years of loyal service in the White House, this nomination was not surprising. Neither was the reaction of Senate Republicans. They refused to bring her nomination up for a vote—one of the few times when Republicans united in completely shutting down a judicial nomination during Clinton's eight years in office. After her nomination languished, Kagan returned to academia and joined the faculty at her alma mater.

Kagan's academic writings at Harvard showed her to be a person of the left, and likely to carry that orientation to the dean's office. In a 2001 article in the *Harvard Law Review,* she praised the Clinton administration's increased use of regulation to implement through the bureaucracy what the president could not persuade Congress to pass through legislation. Kagan, who had helped spearhead the Clinton administration's settlement negotiations with the tobacco industry, made the case for vigorous use of the administrative-litigation arm of the federal bureaucracy. She argued that reliance on such tactics "expanded dramatically during the Clinton years, making the regulatory activity of the executive branch agencies more and more an extension of the President's own policy and political agenda." She explained,

> Faced for most of his time in office with a hostile Congress but eager to show progress on domestic issues, Clinton and his White House staff turned to the bureaucracy to achieve, to the extent it could, the full panoply of his domestic policy goals. Whether the subject was health care, welfare reform, tobacco, or guns, a self-conscious and central object of the White House was to devise, direct, and/or finally announce administrative actions ... to showcase and advance presidential policies.

Still, like Laurence Tribe, Kagan seemed to have written articles with political career advancement in mind. Unlike Frank Michelman or Lani Guinier, she avoided staking out principled positions on contentious issues. Her preference was to write about relatively dull subjects or simply analyze the state of the law rather than express an opinion on the rulings she examined.

Given Kagan's career and politics, few were surprised when her appointment as dean produced a rapturous response from the law school community. After Summers introduced Kagan in the storied Ropes Gray Room in Pound Hall, he was interrupted by applause and cheering for more than a minute. Upon taking the podium, Kagan gushed: "I am honored. I am humbled. And I am thrilled, ecstatic, exhilarated, overjoyed."

Summers' choice of Kagan helped to pacify members of the faculty who found his selection methods overbearing. After Clark announced his resignation from the dean's office, Summers convened a meeting of the Harvard Law faculty and

declared flatly, "The president is charged with sole responsibility to appoint a dean." He then handpicked a committee of
reliable advisors to consider replacement candidates. One professor, Richard Parker, questioned the notion of "trust[ing]
one enlightened president" instead of the law school faculty
for making such a selection. One professor branded Summers
a "control freak." Another professor bluntly denounced Summers as a "tyrant," even while ultimately praising his selection
of Elena Kagan.

Kagan herself elicited nothing but encomia from her colleagues. Martha Field lauded her as a "consensus choice"—a
fair description given the leftward politics at the school. Field
also recalled that Kagan had played the political game well
during her years at Harvard. "She didn't join in all the women's
stuff and we didn't make her because we wanted her to look
more mainstream," Field admitted.

Other observers saw this as one more sign of Harvard's
estrangement from the rest of the country. The school had just
selected as dean a partisan liberal activist who had worked
closely with a president impeached for trying to subvert the
laws he had sworn to uphold as chief executive. That Harvard
had elevated to the deanship someone who had, at some level,
facilitated such high-level misconduct was extraordinary.
Observers were left to speculate on the outcry that would have
occurred had one of Richard Nixon's staff attorneys been
appointed dean of a southern law school in the mid-1970s after
Watergate.

Field believed that Kagan would inspire more trust than
Clark, and that "everyone may calm down" in terms of diversity issues and related hiring squabbles. Nevertheless, Field
expressed concern that female applicants to the Harvard Law
faculty were still being given the shaft. She noted in the spring

of 2003 that over the last four years, the faculty hiring committee had considered seven women but hired only three, even as the last dozen men brought before the committee had all been hired. Field declared this the result of "unconscious prejudice" and expressed her belief that Kagan would help to address this. Another professor, Martha Minow, likewise warned that in the tenure battles, "the power struggles aren't over yet."

FALL 2003 BEGAN THE THIRD and final year for those students who, as 1Ls, had experienced the racial turmoil touched off by Kiwi Camara's class notes. The previous spring, Martha Field and Frank Michelman had expressed their desire and intention to submit the Diversity Committee's report by the end of the 2002–03 academic year. Both wished to finish the job and move on to other matters. (Dean Clark had conscripted all the professors for this unsought and time-intensive duty.) But students returned from summer break to find that the committee still had not released its report and recommendations. The delay was starting to look political.

On September 18, the *Record* noted there was now an "expected fall release date for the report." The paper added, "There may be less bite to the report than some students were expecting, however. Several committee members have said they would be surprised if any speech code emerged out of the report, something many students, most adamantly the Black Law Students Association, have been pushing the Law School to enact." Asked about the status of the report on October 13, 2003, Professor Michelman said it appeared that the report would not be out "before Thanksgiving." Thanksgiving passed and no report was issued. Michelman then said the report "certainly" would be completed by the end of the academic year.

Yet as the school year progressed and the students who had been 1Ls during the tempestuous spring of 2002 neared graduation, still no report emerged from the Diversity Committee. Professor Field acknowledged candidly her perception of the administration's posture toward the pending recommendations. "I think the new dean didn't really want it," she observed. Field, like most faculty members, wanted to see Kagan succeed, and she concluded that withholding the report for a while would allow for a "warming-up period" for the new dean. "We sort of felt we'd let her have her time," Field remarked in the spring of 2004.

Lingering controversy over the Solomon Amendment also blew up in the 2003–04 academic year, competing with the speech-code campaign for the attention and energy of the Harvard Law left. On October 6, 2003, several days after military recruiters began to arrive on campus for interviews, Dean Kagan sent out an e-mail to members of the law-school community. It carried the tone of a segregationist politician apologizing to white constituents for having to afford blacks equal access to public facilities.

Kagan attempted to yoke Dean Clark with much of the blame. It was Clark, she noted, who had lifted the prior "nondiscrimination" policy. "I left this exception in force this year," she said, out of fear of "the enormous adverse impact a prohibition of military recruitment would have on the research and educational missions of other parts of the University." Kagan emphasized that she was personally appalled by the "don't ask, don't tell" policy. "I abhor the military's discriminatory recruitment policy," she stressed. It was "repugnant," "a profound wrong—a moral injustice of the first order." All this angst, it should be recalled, was directed at a federal law that simply required universities to give military recruiters an equal opportunity to speak to prospective officers on their campuses—this in time of war.

The dispute over the Solomon Amendment dominated the political conversation at the law school through the rest of the academic year. In the fall of 2003, a coalition of law schools and professors filed suit and sought an injunction against the U.S. Department of Defense and other federal agencies to block enforcement of the Solomon Amendment. When Harvard declined to join these other schools, Kagan again reiterated the law school's commitment to nondiscrimination. In conversations with gay-rights advocates at the law school, however, she spun the issue as being beyond her control. "Kagan has indicated to me that the decision was made 'above' her, such that I'm more angry at President Summers than the Dean," commented Amanda Goad, president of Lambda, Harvard Law's leading gay-rights organization.

Kagan lent an implicit endorsement to the anti-Solomon forces by encouraging attendance, and speaking herself, at a Lambda-sponsored conference protesting the federal law. The name of the conference was "Solomon's Minefield: Military Discrimination after *Lawrence* [*v. Texas*] and the Coming Fight over Forced On-Campus Recruiting." On October 10, 2003, Kagan appeared before the conference and again passed the buck. "In the end it is the university's decision," she demurred. "I am just a part of the Harvard administration." Yet she repeated her personal disdain for the amendment, attacking the free-speech provisions of a law that her audience characterized as "forced on-campus recruiting."

Like her predecessor in the dean's office, Kagan had come down as an opponent of free speech for military recruiters. She blamed an overzealous Bush administration for implementing the equal-access provisions of the Solomon

Amendment. One conservative law student noted in an opinion piece for the *Record* how, in her mass e-mail advertising the Lambda conference, Kagan had overstepped her bounds: "Effectively Dean Kagan has invited the entire School to an anti-Solomon rally, where she will in fact deliver the official Welcoming Remarks." He further observed, "If a politically conservative Dean ... dispatched an e-mail explaining Harvard's student health facilities but interspersing her explanation with heated criticism of the 'morally unjust,' 'repugnant' realities of abortion, many students and faculty would react with expected vigor ... and I suspect that Lambda would not dissuade them."

The upshot of this clamor over the Solomon Amendment was that many of the school's speech-code agitators became embroiled in a second front. This division of forces was another major reason that the crusade for a speech code began to flounder. Nels Peterson, whose Students for Free Speech had been carefully monitoring the speech-code drive, noticed the impact of the military recruitment controversy. "I think the whole Solomon Amendment business may have taken a lot of the steam out of it, in that people have a finite amount of attention to give to a particular issue, and I think it would be fair to say that a number of the people working on the Solomon Amendment were working on the speech code," he said.

Kagan invited student leaders of both left and right to her office for a meeting ostensibly on the Solomon Amendment in the fall of 2003. In her discussion with conservative student leaders, Kagan said she had discerned from public comments that conservatives were concerned about her leadership at the school. The students expressed frustration at the general chilling of free speech, particularly the still-active consideration of a speech code. One participant observed, "She seemed genuinely interested in hearing us out"—though she was careful not to make any commitments about her own future policies or direction.

IN THE END, there would be no report from the Diversity Committee—at least not in the academic year promised by Professor Michelman, and not before Kiwi Camara and his classmates graduated and carried off with them their unique concerns about the previous racial agitations. This worked well for the administration, for any report that might eventually be published would come out when the main actors in the drama were long gone. Indeed, by the spring of 2004 the committee itself had effectively disbanded through attrition, as student members graduated and left the school. When asked why no report had been published in all this time—a period of time far beyond that required for writing even a monumental Supreme Court opinion—Professor Field and her committee offered no explanation other than the press of other business.

It was unclear whether the report was suppressed or died *in utero* from disinterest. For both the administration and most members of the committee, there certainly was an overriding interest in forgetfulness rather than a final reckoning. But by the time Camara and the other students headed off to their new jobs, the outcome of Harvard's most recent battle over free speech was essentially decided. "I think we're not really doing anything on speech," Field said flatly when queried about the status of the report in April 2004. She added, "If we were doing something on speech, we would have by now." Whatever report might come out of committee in the months or years to follow would, almost certainly, be merely an afterthought affirming the existing culture of expression at Harvard rather than a speech code.

Why did the speech-code movement fail when there was such ambivalence about free speech? The principals in the controversy offered different autopsies. Nels Peterson, the student who organized and led Students for Free Speech, concluded that the speech code had "died in committee." Silverglate had predicted the previous spring, "I'll give you odds they won't adopt [a speech code] now because it's out in the open." He noted that unlike the school's sexual harassment policy, which was not widely publicized until it was on the verge of formal adoption, the proposed speech code had brought national ridicule upon Harvard before it was set in place. The public pressure and resulting retreat were "a testament to the aphorism that sunlight is the best disinfectant."

Silverglate speculated that the law school powers-that-be might have decided to "let it fade away" and not issue a report "because they feel they don't want to rile up any of the various competing constituencies here." He stressed that the Diversity Committee was the brainchild of Bob Clark, not Lawrence Summers or Elena Kagan, who inherited the former dean's attempt to compromise with radicals. Silverglate saw the apparently quiet death of the latest speech-code drive as "a good sign." By contrast, he noted that following the Frug-*Revue* controversy, "they had no problem rounding up the whole faculty to implement the speech code. So this is progress."

Dershowitz agreed with Silverglate that public knowledge and skepticism of the administration's plans had placed speech-code proponents on the defensive. After the administration "way overreacted," Dershowitz stated, "the dean should've announced, this is not ... a problem with the university. This is a marketplace of ideas issue. The students who did it have been condemned. End of the issue." Ultimately, informal social sanctions had proved effective. "It's worked. The marketplace has worked.... The African-American students won. The racist students lost."

Charles Fried judged the simple elapsing of time to be the main reason for the demise of the speech-code movement. The passions stirred up by the racially charged incidents of 2002 "kind of melted away"—a consequence, in no small measure, of the Diversity Committee's delay in issuing its report. Fried observed, "There was a big fuss at the time and a big overreaction, and a number of people exploiting the events to pursue their own political agendas. But I think there was a strong skepticism and resistance to it."

Fried also felt that national reaction to the news of a possible speech code at Harvard had an effect. "What we call conservatives—or what the rest of the country calls middle-of-the-road—are less inclined to be cowed by this political correctness mau-mauing," he commented. "There's a kind of moral bullying which just doesn't work anymore."

Such bullying had, in fact, worked spectacularly at Harvard, but not to the point of rewarding campus leftists with a full-blown speech code. The tombstones planted over the careers of Professors Nesson and Rosenberg would remain memorials to what could befall other politically inept or unpopular professors across the country. Moreover, what Fried had called a "hysterical, ridiculous overreaction to a couple of unfortunate incidents" had revealed the extent to which Harvard Law School found itself at odds with the fundamental precepts of American democracy. "Already there are fewer rights at Harvard Law School than in the rest of the world," Silverglate observed.

The likely trajectory of these continuing efforts at censorship was not hard to discern. As Harvard Law mulled over a speech code, events in France underscored the *reductio ad absurdum* and latent dangers of such efforts. In December 2003, the French government worked to forbid French school-children from wearing "conspicuous" religious symbols such as skullcaps for Jewish boys, large crosses, or headscarves for Muslim girls. The French government also fined a magazine for making "denigrating statements" about Beaujolais wine; the offending article alleged that the less expensive variety tasted like a "sort of lightly fermented and alcoholised fruit juice." The magazine had to pay the equivalent of $250,000.

When viewed alongside limitations on free speech in neighboring Canada, where courts had upheld prohibitions on speaking rudely of racial minorities or questioning same-sex marriage, such broad threats to free speech remained a disturbing plan of action for speech-code activists at Harvard Law. At a minimum, the professional decapitations that had befallen wayward students and faculty at Harvard had shown that frank discussion of issues related to race in American academia was already impossible.

In reaction to this trend, free-speech advocates began a national offensive to secure and, in many cases, restore basic liberties to American campuses. By 2004, at least one state legislature was seriously considering an academic bill of rights drafted by David Horowitz to address a long record of ideological discrimination. The bill proposed prohibiting colleges and universities from making employment or tenure decisions based on political or religious beliefs, grading students according to such beliefs, or failing to offer a diversity of viewpoints. One educator summed up the common mindset of the academic establishment when he told a newspaper that while he supported the bill in principle, he had a problem with "the people who've latched on" to it—namely, men of the right such as Horowitz.

Harvard Law's dalliance with a speech code had shown that no institution was safe from this drive, and that the movement to suppress politically incorrect speech was a national one on the brink of success. That such an extreme measure, one antithetical to the most basic premises and traditions of American democracy, was nearly woven into the fabric of America's oldest law school spoke to the broad intellectual support that such policies enjoyed in academia. Law professors who would hunch over their computers for hours devising elaborate defenses for the speech rights of Nazis and child pornographers were silent, almost to a person, in the face of this radical movement to deny basic liberties. As long as Harvard Law remained the legal and cultural powerhouse it had been for decades, the battles over its future would continue to reverberate throughout the nation—and to remind that nation of the direction in which it was headed.

Few believed that the outcome of Harvard Law's speech-code controversy marked an end to the clash over free speech in academia or society. Alan Dershowitz observed, "Every two years or three years [this topic] is going to come up again, and it's going to come up unpredictably, and you never know where it's going to come from."

This conflict, as old as democracy itself, would showcase powerful interests seeking to curb or deny the right of dissent of those in opposition to them. In this, as in so many other respects, Harvard Law School had served as both trendsetter and omen for the American society that had long called upon it for guidance in matters legal and cultural. Justice Scalia had once lamented, "Day by day, case by case, [the Supreme Court] is busy designing a Constitution for a country I do not recognize." Scalia might well have added that the Court was refashioning America according to the intellectual blueprint drafted at his alma mater, now under new and very different leadership that he would also have trouble recognizing.

The U.S. Supreme Court had drawn intellectual inspiration from Harvard Law School for almost two hundred years; that the school would continue to exert such influence was not in doubt. What remained to be seen was whether America's leading law school would reclaim its tradition of celebrating dissent, or instead continue to thwart the very constitutional liberties that once gave the school life and purpose.

ACKNOWLEDGMENTS

This book was jointly inspired by my editor, Peter Collier, and the people of Arizona. During the editing of my last book, *Clarence Thomas,* Peter mentioned in passing one day that he thought a book needed to be written about Harvard Law School. That notion germinated the following year when I ran for attorney general of Arizona. As I shared with audiences my experiences as a conservative at Harvard Law, I observed at once a fascination with and a profound mistrust of that important institution. The voters, in their unchallengeable wisdom, decided not to elect me to that office, but from the experience a book was born.

I am grateful to Roland and Betsy Nehring of the Nehring Foundation and to Len Munsil and the Center for Arizona Policy for their support of this project. Freedom has no more steadfast allies than these generous supporters.

I also wish to thank the professors, students and alumni of Harvard Law School who generously took time from the paper chase to grant interviews. Dean Robert Clark and much of the administration stonewalled me; but that was to be expected, and was in keeping with my memories of the place.

Finally, I owe special thanks to my wife, Ann, and our

children for their patience and liberality in surrendering their husband and father to the ever-beckoning computer while this book was being written.

NOTES

Prologue: Property Crimes

1–6   Camara—Interview of Kiwi Camara; articles in *Harvard Law Record.*

6–12   History of Harvard Law School—Arthur E. Sutherland, *The Law at Harvard: A History of Ideas and Men, 1817–1967* (Cambridge, Mass.: Belknap Press, 1967), pp. 26–44, 101, 147.

10   Turow—Scott Turow, *One L* (New York: Farrar Straus Giroux, 1977), p. 41.

14–16   Unger's philosophy—Roberto Mangabeira Unger, *The Critical Legal Studies Movement* (Cambridge, Mass.: Harvard University Press, 1986), pp. 2, 41, 108–12.

16–17   D. Kennedy biographical—Eleanor Kerlow, *Poisoned Ivy: How Egos, Ideology, and Power Politics Almost Ruined Harvard Law School* (New York: St. Martin's, 1994), pp. 139–44.

17   D. Kennedy writings—Duncan Kennedy, *A Critique of Adjudication (fin de siècle)* (Cambridge, Mass.: Harvard University Press, 1997).

17–18   Gabel-Kennedy article—Peter Gabel and Duncan Kennedy, "Roll Over Beethoven," 36 *Stanford Law Review* 1–55, 4 (1984).

17   "old acid-heads"—David Luban, "Legal Modernism," 84 *Michigan Law Review* 1656–95, 1671 (1986).

18–19   D. Kennedy and janitors—Brian Timmons, "That's No

Okie, That's My Torts Professor," *Wall Street Journal,* April 3, 1990, p. A20.

19–20   Horwitz—Morton Horwitz, *The Transformation of American Law, 1780–1860* (New York: Oxford University Press, 1992), pp. xv–xvi, 107–8; Morton J. Horwitz, *The Warren Court and the Pursuit of Justice* (New York: Hill & Wang, 1998), pp. 8, 80–81.

20–21   Faculty infighting in 1980s—Kerlow, *Poisoned Ivy,* pp. 49–52.

22   Paul Butler—Paul Butler, "Racially Based Jury Nullification: Black Power in the Criminal Justice System," 105 *Yale Law Journal* 677–726, 677–80 (1995).

22   "applied critical race theory"—Jeffrey Rosen, "The Bloods and the Crits," *New Republic,* December 9, 1996, pp. 27–42.

23   *Bakke—Regents of the University of California v. Bakke,* 438 U.S. 265 (1978).

23   Quota system on *Harvard Law Review*—Kerlow, *Poisoned Ivy,* pp. 22–23.

25   "struggle for the soul"—Ibid., p. 23.

26   Holmes—*Abrams v. United States,* 250 U.S. 616, 630, 40 S.Ct. 17 (1919) (Holmes, J., dissenting).

26   Brennan—*New York Times v. Sullivan,* 376 U.S. 254 (1964).

26   Dershowitz—Arthur J. Goldberg and Alan M. Dershowitz, "Declaring the Death Penalty Unconstitutional," 83 *Harvard Law Review* 1773 (1970).

28   Scalia—*Romer v. Evans,* 517 U.S. 620, 116 S.Ct. 1620, 1637 (1996) (Scalia, J., dissenting).

Chapter One: Crocodile Hunting

33–35   Derrick Bell—Eleanor Kerlow, *Poisoned Ivy: How Egos, Ideology, and Power Politics Almost Ruined Harvard Law School* (New York: St. Martin's, 1994), pp. 80–90; Derrick Bell, *Confronting Authority: Reflections of an Ardent Protester* (Boston: Beacon Press, 1994), pp. 29–39.

35–37   Bell's storytelling—Derrick Bell, "The Final Report: Harvard's Affirmative Action Allegory," 87 *Michigan Law Review* 2382–2410 (1989); Derrick Bell, "The Supreme Court, 1984 Term - Foreword: The Civil Rights

Chronicles," 99 *Harvard Law Review* 4–83 (1985–86).

37 Randall Kennedy vs. Bell—Randall L. Kennedy, "Racial Critiques of Legal Academia," 102 *Harvard Law Review* 1745–1819, 1765 (1989).

37 "oppressor class"—Derrick Bell, *Faces at the Bottom of the Well: The Permanence of Racism* (New York: Basic Books, 1992), p. 113.

39 "substantial number of Jewish professors"—Bell, *Confronting Authority,* pp. 76–77.

41 Bell on tokenism—Derrick Bell, "Diversity and Academic Freedom," 43 *Journal of Legal Education* 371–79 (1993).

44–45 "gcrocodile"—*Harvard Law Record* articles. In response to the author's request for an interview, Scholl responded by e-mail, "I regret but I will not be able to accept any interview requests on that topic until after graduation from HLS, presumably in June 2004."

Chapter Two: Up in Smoke

47–48 Nesson and Ellsberg—Tom Wells, *Wild Man: The Life and Times of Daniel Ellsberg* (New York: Palgrave, 2001), pp. 425–32, 441–44, 448–49, 536, 538.

49–50 Nesson in *Civil Action*—Jonathan Harr, *A Civil Action* (New York: Random House, 1995), pp. 235–52.

51–52 Nesson's teaching, drug use—Joseph P. Flood, "The Path Less Traveled," *Harvard Crimson,* April 19, 2002; interviews of Harvard Law faculty.

52 Nesson on 1980s faculty squabbles—Eleanor Kerlow, *Poisoned Ivy: How Egos, Ideology, and Power Politics Almost Ruined Harvard Law School* (New York: St. Martin's, 1994), pp. 49–53.

53–56 Nesson-Scholl on April 4—Jennifer L. Steinhardt, "Epithet Garners Apology," *Harvard Law Record,* April 5, 2002; interviews of Harvard Law students.

Chapter Three: The Limits of Tenure

58–61 Background on Rosenberg—Interview of Harvey Silverglate.

59–60 Rosenberg on tort law—David Rosenberg, "Individual

Justice and Collectivizing Risk-Based Claims in Mass-Exposure Cases," 71 *New York University Law Review* 210–57 (April-May 1996); David Rosenberg, "The Path Not Taken," 110 *Harvard Law Review* 1044–1048 (1997).

61–63   Rosenberg incidents—Tamar Lewin, "Comments Concerning Race Divide Harvard Law School," *New York Times,* April 20, 2002; *Harvard Law Record* articles; interview of Nels Peterson; Jeffrey Toobin, "Speechless," *New Yorker,* January 27, 2003, pp. 32–39.

Chapter Four: Boneless Bob

65–66   History of Black Law Students Association—Lewis Rice, "A Generation Apart, a Common Goal," *Harvard Law Bulletin,* Fall 2000.

66–67   BLSA letter—*Harvard Law Record* articles.

67–69   BLSA rally—Ibid.

69–70   Background on Cornel West—Cornel West, "The Making of an American Radical Democrat of African Descent," in *The Cornel West Reader* (New York: Basic Books, 1999), pp. 3–18, dedication page.

70   West on Marxism after Soviet breakup—Cornel West, *The Ethical Dimensions of Marxist Thought* (New York: Monthly Review Press, 1991), p. xiv.

70–71   Wieseltier on West—Leon Wieseltier, "All and Nothing at All," *New Republic,* March 6, 1995, pp. 31–36.

71   West-Summers feud—Pam Belluck with Jacques Steinberg, "Defector Indignant at President of Harvard," *New York Times,* April 16, 2002, p. A24; John McWhorter, "Cornel West Gives Black Scholars a Bad Rap," *Wall Street Journal,* April 16, 2002; Timothy Noah, "Cornel West Whine Watch," www.slate.msn.com, posted April 16, 2002.

72   Ogletree assuming Bell's role—Derrick Bell, *Confronting Authority: Reflections of an Ardent Protester* (Boston: Beacon Press, 1994), p. 69.

72–73   Ogletree on reparations—Charles J. Ogletree Jr., "The Case for Reparations," *USA Weekend Magazine,* August 18, 2002.

73   Ogletree and *Harvard Law Review*—Eleanor Kerlow,

Poisoned Ivy: How Egos, Ideology, and Power Politics Almost Ruined Harvard Law School (New York: St. Martin's, 1994), p. 305.

73–74   Ogletree on criminal justice system—Charles J. Ogletree Jr., "The Burdens and Benefits of Race in America," 25 *Hastings Constitutional Law Quarterly* 217–54, 230–47 (Winter 1998).

74–75   Ogletree on hate speech—Charles J. Ogletree Jr., "The Limits of Hate Speech: Does Race Matter?" 32 *Gonzaga Law Review* 491–510, 496–99, 509 (1996–97).

75–78   Clark biographical—Kerlow, *Poisoned Ivy,* pp. 133, 139–50; Harvard Law website: www.law.harvard.edu/faculty.

78   Clark "backpedals"—Kerlow, *Poisoned Ivy,* p. 147.

78   "most recent cycle"—Interview of Alan Dershowitz.

79–80   Frug article—Mary Joe Frug, "A Postmodern Feminist Legal Manifesto (An Unfinished Draft)," 105 *Harvard Law Review* 1045–1075, 1072–73 (1992).

79–86   Frug-*Revue* controversy—Peter Collier, "Blood on the Charles," *Vanity Fair,* October 1992, pp. 144–64.

80–83   Fried—Interview of Charles Fried; Charles Fried, *Order and Law: Arguing the Reagan Revolution—A Firsthand Account* (New York: Simon & Schuster, 1991), pp. 13–14, 20; Charles Fried, *Contract As Promise: A Theory of Contractual Obligation* (Cambridge, Mass.: Harvard University Press, 1981), p. i; Kerlow, *Poisoned Ivy,* pp. 158–59; *Lawrence v. Texas,* 123 S.Ct. 2742, 2483 (2003) (citing Fried's *Order and Law*).

84–86   Silverglate—Interview of Harvey Silverglate.

86–89   Administration's actions after April 15 rally—Jennifer L. Steinhardt, "Incidents Draw Law School Response," *Harvard Crimson,* April 10, 2002; interviews of Harvard Law faculty.

88   *McIntyre v. Ohio Elections Commission*—514 U.S. 334, 115 S.Ct. 1511 (1995).

Chapter Five: Triumph of the Crits

91–92   Nesson and Rakoff—Owen Alterman, "Nesson Says Rakoff Suggested He Remove Himself from Teaching

1Ls," *Harvard Law Record,* April 25, 2002.

92–96   Nesson and Rosenberg—Joseph P. Flood, "Nesson Steps Down from Teaching amid Protests," *Harvard Crimson,* April 22, 2002.

96–97   Dershowitz "keeps the brand strong"—Interview of Jonathan Skrmetti.

97   Dershowitz vs. Cockburn battle—Alexander Cockburn, "Alan Dershowitz, Plagiarist," *Counterpunch,* September 26, 2003, www.counterpunch.org; Eric Marx, "Dershowitz Rebuts Critics' Plagiarism Charges," *The Forward,* October 3, 2003, www.forward.com.

98–99   Dershowitz on hate speech—Alan M. Dershowitz, *The Abuse Excuse: And Other Cop-Outs, Sob Stories, and Evasions of Responsibility* (Boston: Little, Brown, 1994), pp. 260–64.

99   Dershowitz on Clinton, *Bush v. Gore*—Alan M. Dershowitz, *Sexual McCarthyism: Clinton, Starr, and the Emerging Constitutional Crisis* (New York: Basic Books, 1998), p. 198; Alan M. Dershowitz, *Supreme Injustice: How the High Court Hijacked Election 2000* (Oxford: Oxford University Press, 2001), p. 3.

99–100   Treatment of Rosenberg troubles faculty—Interviews of Harvard Law faculty.

100–1   Background on Rosenberg—Interview of Harvey Silverglate.

Chapter Six: Diversity, Harvard Style

103–5   September changes—Clinton Dick, "HLS Responds to Racial Incidents," *Harvard Law Record,* September 19, 2002.

105–6   "Difficult Conversations" materials—Provided by Harvey Silverglate.

107   Silverglate-Clark correspondence—Interview of Harvey Silverglate.

107   Guinier becomes HLS race counselor—Patrick Healy, "Harvard Law Plan on Speech Causes Stir," *Boston Globe,* November 19, 2002, p. A1.

108–9   Guinier on political system, affirmative action—Lani Guinier, *The Tyranny of the Majority: Fundamental Fair-*

ness in Representative Democracy (New York: Free
Press, 1994), pp. 12–17, 117; Lani Guinier, "Confirmative
Action," 25 *Law & Social Inquiry* 565–83 (2000).

110   Field's writings—Martha A. Field, "Abortion and the
First Amendment," 29 *University of California, Davis
Law Review* 545–51, 550–51 (1996).

111   Dershowitz as "ballast"—Interview of Frank
Michelman.

111   Michelman's "empathy"—Derrick Bell, *Confronting
Authority: Reflections of an Ardent Protester* (Boston:
Beacon Press, 1994), p. 65.

111–13   Michelman's writings—Frank I. Michelman, "Reason,
Passion and the Progress of Law: Remembering and
Advancing the Constitutional Vision of Justice William J.
Brennan," 33 *Harvard Civil Rights–Civil Liberties Law
Review* 317–20, 318–19 (1998); Frank I. Michelman,
"Brennan and Democracy," 86 *California Law Review*
399–427, 399, 426–27 (1998); Frank I. Michelman, "Con-
stitutional Authorship by the People," 74 *Notre Dame
Law Review* 1605–29, 1629 (1999); Frank I. Michelman,
"'Protecting the People from Themselves,' or How
Direct Can Democracy Be?" 45 *UCLA Law Review*
1717–1734 (1998).

113   "Warren Court baby"—Interview of Frank Michelman.

114–15   Edley's writings—Christopher Edley Jr., *Not All Black
and White: Affirmative Action, Race, and American Values* (New York: Hill & Wang, 1996), pp. 80, 212, 278.

115–16   Bartholet—Interview of Elizabeth Bartholet.

Chapter Seven: "Conservatives Should Shut Up about Silencing"

118   Conservative complaints to committee—Interview of
Martha Field.

118–19   "religious radicalism"—Arthur E. Sutherland, *The Law
at Harvard: A History of Ideas and Men, 1817–1967*
(Cambridge, Mass.: Belknap Press, 1967), pp. 79–80.

121–24   Accounts of liberal intolerance at Harvard Law—Interviews of Nels Peterson, Jonathan Skrmetti, Katie Biber,
Carrie Campbell.

123   *Harvard Law Bulletin* article—Jonas Blank, "All the
        Right's Moves," *Harvard Law Bulletin*, Spring 2003,
        pp. 18–22.

124–26 Study in *Wall Street Journal*—John O. McGinnis and
        Matthew Schwartz, "Conservatives Need Not Apply,"
        Wall Street Journal, April 1, 2003, p. A14.

126   Fried—Interview of Charles Fried.

126–27 Dershowitz on true diversity—Eleanor Kerlow,
        *Poisoned Ivy: How Egos, Ideology, and Power Politics
        Almost Ruined Harvard Law School* (New York: St.
        Martin's, 1994), p. 272.

127–28 Absence of originalists, pro-life professors—Interviews
        of Martha Field, Charles Fried, Frank Michelman.

128–29 Stephan Thernstrom—Dinesh D'Souza, *Illiberal Educa-
        tion: The Politics of Race and Sex on Campus* (New
        York: Free Press, 1991), pp. 194–97; interview of Stephan
        Thernstrom.

130   Hanson—Steve P. Croley and Jon D. Hanson, "The Non-
        pecuniary Costs of Accidents: Pain-and-Suffering Dam-
        ages in Tort Law," 108 *Harvard Law Review* 1785–1917
        (1995); interview of Carrie Campbell.

130–31 Singer—Interview of Katie Biber.

131   *Record* editorial—Editorial, "Conservatives Should Shut
        Up about Silencing," *Harvard Law Record*, March 13,
        2003.

Chapter Eight: Poetic Injustice

135–36 Paulin flap—Alexander J. Blenkinsopp, "Poet Flap Drew
        Summers' Input," *Harvard Crimson*, November 14, 2002.

137   Bork on Tribe—Robert H. Bork, *The Tempting of Amer-
        ica: The Political Seduction of the Law* (New York: Free
        Press, 1990, p. 199.

137–38 Other conservatives on Tribe—Quoted in Eleanor Ker-
        low, *Poisoned Ivy: How Egos, Ideology, and Power Poli-
        tics Almost Ruined Harvard Law School* (New York: St.
        Martin's, 1994), p. 242.

138   Tribe on Clinton—Laurence H. Tribe, "Defining 'High
        Crimes and Misdemeanors,'" Testimony before Con-

gress, in 67 *George Washington Law Review* 712–734, 723–25 (1999).

139–41   Dershowitz vs. Tribe—Peter Collier, "Blood on the Charles," *Vanity Fair,* October 1992; Kerlow, *Poisoned Ivy,* pp. 243–64.

142   Letter of Dershowitz, Fried and Tribe—"Withdrawing Paulin's Invitation Unnecessary," *Harvard Crimson,* November 15, 2002.

143–44   Tribe stays out of racial harassment code—Tribe's e-mail to the author dated February 2, 2003; second e-mail from Tribe to the author dated May 26, 2003.

Chapter Nine: The Socratic Method Becomes a Hate Crime

145   Field's comments—Jonas Blank, "Harassment Policy Proposal Draws Fire," *Harvard Law Record,* November 21, 2002.

146   Pound vs. Frankfurter—Eleanor Kerlow, *Poisoned Ivy: How Egos, Ideology, and Power Politics Almost Ruined Harvard Law School* (New York: St. Martin's, 1994), pp. 2–3.

148–51   Randall Kennedy's writings—Randall Kennedy, *Interracial Intimacies: Sex, Marriage, Identity, and Adoption* (New York: Pantheon, 2003), pp. 36–37, 401–2, 411; Randall Kennedy, *Nigger: The Strange Career of a Troublesome Word* (New York: Pantheon, 2002), pp. 117, 122–23, 142–58.

152   Kilson vs. R. Kennedy—"Former Harvard Professor Blasts 'Nigger' Book," www.bet.com, posted July 2, 2002.

152–53   Dershowitz vs. R. Kennedy—Interview of Alan Dershowitz; Patrick Healy, "Harvard Law Plan on Speech Causes Stir," *Boston Globe,* November 19, 2002, p. A1.

154   Hissing of Fielding—Interview of Nels Peterson.

156   Clark's resignation—Mike Wiser, "Clark Announces Resignation," *Harvard Law Record,* November 25, 2002 (posted online).

157   Praise of Clark—Lewis Rice, "The Man of the Moment," *Harvard Law Bulletin,* Summer 2003, pp. 10–17.

Chapter Ten: Worlds Apart

159–60   Background on Lawrence, Matsuda and Delgado—Alan
          Charles Kors and Harvey A. Silverglate, *The Shadow
          University: The Betrayal of Liberty on America's Cam-
          puses* (New York: Free Press, 1998), p. 72.

160–61   Seminal writings of Lawrence, Matsuda and Delgado—
          Richard Delgado, "Storytelling for Oppositionists and
          Others: A Plea for Narrative," 87 *Michigan Law Review*
          2411 (1989); Charles Lawrence III, "If He Hollers Let
          Him Go: Racist Speech on Campus," *Duke Law Journal*
          (June 1990): 431–83; Mari J. Matsuda, "Public Response
          to Racist Speech: Considering the Victim's Story," 87
          Michigan Law Review 2320–81 (August 1989); Richard
          Delgado, "Words That Wound: A Tort Action for Racial
          Insults, Epithets and Name-Calling," 17 *Harvard Civil
          Rights–Civil Liberties Law Review* 133–81 (Spring 1982).

    161   *Chaplinsky v. New Hampshire* and its progeny—315 U.S.
          568, 62 S.Ct. 766 (1942); *Brandenburg v. Ohio,* 395 U.S.
          444, 89 S.Ct. 1827 (1969); *R.A.V. v. St. Paul,* 505 U.S. 377,
          112 S.Ct. 2538 (1992).

161–62   Michigan and Wisconsin speech codes—*Doe v. Univer-
          sity of Michigan,* 721 F.Supp. 852 (E.D. Mich. 1989);
          *UWM Post v. Board of Regents of the University of Wis-
          consin,* 774 F.Supp. 1163 (E.D. Wis. 1991).

162–63   Allan Bloom—Allan Bloom, *The Closing of the Ameri-
          can Mind: How Higher Education Has Failed Democracy
          and Impoverished the Souls of Today's Students* (New
          York: Simon & Schuster, 1987), pp. 91–92.

    163   Poll and remarks of black student leaders—Vasugi V.
          Ganeshananthan, "The Comfort Zone," *Harvard Crim-
          son,* April 25, 2002.

    165   Students for Free Speech—Interview of Nels Peterson.

    165   Letter to *Record*—Austin W. Bramwell, Letter to the
          Editor, *Harvard Law Record,* February 6, 2003.

165–68   Ostracism of Camara and Scholl—Interviews of Kiwi
          Camara and Harvard Law students.

Chapter Eleven: Un-Martial Law

169–70   September 11 discussions—Interviews of Jonathan

Skrmetti, Nels Peterson; J. R. Parker, "Foreign Engagement Got Us Here," *Harvard Law Record,* September 21, 2001; Clifford Ginn, "Don't Sacrifice Freedom for Security," *Harvard Law Record,* September 21, 2001; Mike Wiser, "Divided Faculty Panel Debates U.S. Response to Global Terror," *Harvard Law Record,* September 27, 2001.

171   Background on Solomon Amendment—Lee Bockhorn, "The Wisdom of Solomon," *Daily Standard,* November 8, 2002, www.weeklystandard.com.

172–73   Gay rights rally—Jonas Blank, "Students, Faculty, Administrators Rally against 'Don't Ask, Don't Tell,'" *Harvard Law Record,* October 10, 2002.

173–75   Janet Halley's writings—Janet E. Halley, "Sexual Orientation and the Politics of Biology: A Critique of the Argument from Immutability," 46 *Stanford Law Review* 505–68, 505–06, 568 (1993–94); *Lawrence v. Texas,* 123 S.Ct. at 2478–81 (discussion of history of sodomy laws and relationship to nonprocreative sexual activity).

175   Halley on "private institution"—Interview of Janet Halley.

176   Poll of Harvard students on war—Nalina Sombuntham, "Crimson Poll: Majority against Military Action," *Harvard Crimson,* March 21, 2003.

176–77   Administration's reaction to war—Clinton Dick, "Iraq War, HLS Reacts," *Harvard Law Record,* March 20, 2003.

Chapter Twelve: Breaking the Code

179–81   Diversity Committee considers options—Interviews of Martha Field, Frank Michelman; e-mail from Frank Michelman, December 5, 2003.

180   *Virginia v. Black*—123 S.Ct. 1536, 1547–48 (2003).

181   Summers' personality conflicts—Matt Feeney, "West of Everything," *National Review Online,* www.nationalreview.com, posted August 13, 2002.

182   "Difficult Conversations" fizzles—George Hicks, "'Difficult Conversations' Didn't Seem to Happen," Letter to the Editor, *Harvard Law Record,* March 20, 2003.

182–83   Reynolds' letter—Terry Eastland, "Breaking the Code," *Daily Standard,* September 2, 2003, www.weeklystandard.com.

184–85   Kagan's scholarship—Elena Kagan, "Presidential Administration," 114 *Harvard Law Review* 2245–2385, 2248 (2001).

186   Field on Kagan—Interview of Martha Field.

187   Minow on continuing troubles—James Traub, "Harvard Radical," *New York Times Magazine,* August 24, 2003, sect. 6, p. 28.

187–88   Delay in Diversity Committee report—Interviews of Martha Field and Frank Michelman; "News Briefs: Expected Fall Release of Healthy Diversity Report," *Harvard Law Record,* September 18, 2003.

188–91   Solomon Amendment controversy—E-mail from Dean Elena Kagan, October 6, 2003; Clinton Dick, "Kagan States Her Case before Lambda," *Harvard Law Record,* October 16, 2003; Adam White, "Save Your Solomonic Judgment, Dean," *Harvard Law Record,* October 9, 2003.

191–92   Speech-code drive flounders—Interview of Nels Peterson.

192–93   Analysis of committee work—Interviews of Alan Dershowitz, Charles Fried, Harvey Silverglate.

194   French magazine—David Frum's Diary, *National Review Online,* www.nationalreview.com, posted March 7, 2003.

194   Horowitz legislation—Amanda Paulson, "A Bill to Protect Campus Conservatives?" *Christian Science Monitor,* January 8, 2004.

195   Scalia—Quoted in Robert H. Bork, "Whose Constitution Is It, Anyway?" *National Review,* December 8, 2003, p. 37.

INDEX

abortion, 123, 128
Abrams v. United States, 26
"academic bill of rights," 194
academic rigor, 9–11; decline of,
    22–23
affirmative action, 23, 25, 75, 98,
    124; Bell on, 35–39; in faculty
    hiring, 32–42, 50–51, 181–82;
    Fried on, 128; Guinier on,
    108–9; Harvard Civil Rights
    Project, 114; and Jews, 39;
    Supreme Court on, 114; for
    women, 39–41
American Civil Liberties
    Union, 27, 78, 113, 133
American Constitutional Law
    (Tribe), 137
American Enterprise Institute,
    115
anti-Americanism, 169–70
anti-Semitism, 45, 135–37,
    142–43
antiwar protests, 65, 170, 175–77
Aquinas, Thomas, 11
Association of Black Harvard
    Women, 163

Austin, John, 11
Austin, Regina, 39–40; as
    "token token," 41

Bailyn, Bernard, 129
Bakker, Jim, 97
Bankole, Olunfunke Grace, 44
Bartholet, Elizabeth, 84, 115–16
Bator, Paul, 21
Bell, Derrick, 33–43, 71, 107,
    113, 119, 146, 147–48; on
    affirmative action, 35–40;
    bitter legacy of, 42–43;
    BLSA support of, 65, 66;
    complaints about, 34–35; Crit
    support for, 42; on faculty
    hiring standards, 35–42; fac-
    ulty support of, 42; and
    Fried, 82–83; at Justice
    Dept., 33; lack of qualifica-
    tions, 34, 38; leave of
    absence, 41–42, 111; at
    NAACP, 33; and Nesson,
    50–51; at New York U., 41;
    on Ogletree, 72; at Oregon,
    34; "politically correct"

Bell, Derrick (cont.)
award, 79–80; on "race traitors," 37–38, 98, 152, 153; on
separatism, 162; at Stanford,
34–35; storytelling style,
35–37, 160; on tokenism, 41
Bell, Robert, 34
Benchmark, 137–38
Biber, Katie, 121–22, 130–31,
133
bin Laden, Osama, 170
Black Entertainment Television, 71
Black Law Students Associa-
tion (BLSA), 34, 101, 106;
appeasement of, 86–87; and
Bell, 65, 66; on Camara inci-
dent, 66–68; demands of,
66–67, 147, 159; Legal Aid
Bureau incident, 66; origins,
65–66; rally by, 67–69; speech
code campaign, 67, 86–87,
147, 151, 152, 154–55, 162,
163, 187
Black Men's Forum, 163
Black Panthers, 162
Blackstone, William, 6–7
Bloom, Allan, 115; on sepa-
ratism, 162–63
*Bluebook: A Uniform System of
Citation,* 80
Boies, David, 138
Bok, Derek, 34, 36, 65
Bork, Robert, 137, 141
Brandeis, Louis, 9
Brawley, Tawana, 149
Brennan, William, 19–20, 112;
on First Amendment, 26, 113
Breyer, Stephen, 31

Buell, Lawrence, 136, 142
Bush v. Gore, 27, 99, 136, 138
Butler, Paul, 22
Byrne, W. Matthew, 48

Calero, Adolfo, 119
Camara, Kiwi, 1–6; class outlines posted, 3–5, 29, 85;
clerkship, 167; complaints
against, 5, 43–44, 61, 66–68;
graduation, 191; immaturity,
3–4; official action on, 87–88;
opportunities lost, 167–68,
179; as outsider/eccentric, 3,
166; as prodigy, 1–2; racial
slurs, 4–5; shunning of, 165–
68, 179; threats against, 166
Campbell, Carrie, 124
Canada, 194
Carter, Jimmy, 113
Carville, James, 173
Cary-Sadler, Tel, 62–63, 95
Case for Israel, The
(Dershowitz), 97
case-study method, 10–11
Chaplinsky v. New Hampshire,
161–62
Cheney, Dick, 172
Civil Action, A (book/film), 49
Civil Procedure class, 120
Civil Rights Act of 1964, 23, 75
"Civil Rights Chronicles, The"
(Bell), 36–37
Clark, Robert, 2, 40, 42, 52,
75–78, 92, 146; appeasement
& waffling, 78, 85–89, 101,
155–57; BLSA demands on,
66, 68; as "conservative," 75,
76–78, 128; on Critical Legal

Studies, 76–77; Difficult Conversations program, 104–7; and Diversity Committee, 87–89, 103–4, 115, 187, 192; faculty workshops, 107, 109; and Frug-*Revue* controversy, 83–86, 115; material accomplishments, 156; on military recruitment, 171–72, 175, 188; on Ogletree, 77, 78; ouster of, 115, 139; "racial harassment policy," 86–89; resigns deanship, 156; social engineering, 107; speech code plans, 87, 89, 94, 104–5
Clinton, Bill, 99, 113–14; "don't ask, don't tell" policy, 175; impeachment, 138, 184, 186; scandals, 138, 184
Coalition for Civil Rights, 40
Cochran, Johnnie, 22
Cockburn, Alexander, 97
Committee on Healthy Diversity. *See* Diversity Committee
Committee on Multicultural Unity, 118, 122
Commonwealth v. Amirault, 82
Conner, Harrel E., 163
conservatives, 117–33, 193; and "academic bill of rights," 194; and Camara, 166–67; dearth on faculty, 25, 124–31; double standard toward, 132; grievances of, 117–18, harassment of, 121–23, 163–64; *Harvard Law Bulletin* article on, 123; and indoctrination, 119–21; isolation of, 128–30; self-censorship, 122, 124,

125–26, 131, 132; on speech codes, 117, 131, 163–65, 190–91
Contracts As Promise (Fried), 81
Contracts class, 120
Criminal Law class, 120–21
Crimson, The, 142, 163, 176
Critical Legal Studies & "Crits," 13–23, 29, 91–101, 111, 119, 124, 160; branches of, 21; Clark's appeasement of, 87, 101, 156–57; Clark's criticism of, 76–77; and declining standards, 22–23; and deconstruction, 13, 18; dominance of, 24–26, 87, 91–101, 157; and faculty appointments, 20–21, 24–25, 42, 60; Federalist Society debate on, 76; in Frug-*Revue* controversy, 79–80, 84; and liberation theology, 14; nihilism of, 60, 77; opposition to, 60–63; Rosenberg's criticism of, 60–63, 93–94, 100–1; support of Bell, 42
Critical Queer Theory, 21, 173–74
Critical Race Theory, 21–22; on jury nullification, 22; and speech codes, 150–51
Cruise, Tom, 28

Dalton, Clare, 60, 77, 94
Dambrot, Keith, 150
Davis, Angela, 73
Dean's Committee on Healthy Diversity. *See* Diversity Committee

death penalty, 26–27
Delgado, Richard, 150, 159–60,
     161
Derrida, Jacques, 13
Dershowitz, Alan, 24, 26, 37, 78,
     96–101, 137; on affirmative
     action, 98; ambition/prestige,
     96–97; on Bell, 98; as civil
     libertarian, 98–100, 111; as
     defense attorney, 96–97; on
     Diversity Committee, 111;
     earnings, 141; on Frug-*Revue*
     controversy, 98–99, 139–41;
     on intellectual diversity,
     126–27; and Jewish causes,
     97, 98; on Nesson, 99–100; on
     Paulin case, 136, 139, 141–43;
     plagiarism accusation, 97; on
     Rosenberg, 101; on social
     sanctions, 192–93; on
     Solomon Amendment, 173;
     on speech codes, 99–100, 115,
     145–46, 147, 152–53, 154–55,
     192, 195; on tenure, 101; vs.
     Tribe, 139–41
"Difficult Conversations" pro-
     gram, 104–7, 182; publicity,
     106–7
Diversity Committee ("Com-
     mittee on Healthy Diver-
     sity"), 87–89, 103–7; as
     Clark's project, 87–89, 103–4,
     115, 192; and conservative
     grievances, 118, 121; final
     report pending, 187–88, 191;
     members of, 109–16; name
     change, 145; policy options,
     104–5, 145, 179–82; on

speech code, 115–16, 145,
     147, 150–55
Diversity Town Hall meeting,
     145–54
Dukakis, Michael, 113

Edley, Christopher, 83, 87,
     113–15, 140, 179; on affirma-
     tive action, 114–15; as politi-
     cal operative, 113–14
Ellsberg, Carol, 48
Ellsberg, Daniel, 47–48
Emancipation Proclamation, 75
English Department
     (Harvard), 135–36, 142–43
*Ethical Dimensions of Marxist
     Thought, The* (West), 70
existentialism, 13

"Faces at the Bottom of the
     Well" (Bell), 37
faculty hiring & tenure, 19–20,
     77; affirmative action in,
     32–42, 50–51, 181–82; and
     Crits, 20–21, 24–25, 42, 60;
     discrimination lawsuit,
     40–41; of women, 38, 39–41,
     186–87
Farrakhan, Louis, 39
Federalist Society, 76, 82, 126,
     166–67
Fells Acres Day School, 82
feminism, 62, 79; and Fem-Crit
     Studies, 21, 62
Few Good Men, A (film), 28
Field, Martha, 83, 104, 110–11,
     113, 118, 128, 132; on Diver-
     sity Committee aims, 145,

179–80, 187–88, 191; on First Amendment, 110; on hiring women, 186–87; on Kagan, 186; on *Roe v. Wade,* 110
"fighting words" doctrine, 161
"Final Report, The" (Bell), 35
Firm, The (film), 28
First Amendment, 26, 54, 74, 84, 85, 180–83; anonymous speech, 87, 88, 165; on cross burning, 180; Dershowitz on, 98; and group-identity politics, 160–62; *New York Times v. Sullivan,* 113; at private institutions, 44, 145, 175, 181; and *Roe v. Wade,* 110; *Virginia v. Black,* 180; *see also* speech codes
Florida State University Law Review, 79
Foucault, Michel, 13
Foundation for Individual Rights in Education, 58, 165
France, 193–94
Frankfurter, Felix, 9, 146
Fried, Charles, 27, 126; affirmative action criticism, 128; on Bell, 82–83; in *Commonwealth v. Amirault,* 82; as "conservative," 80–83; and Federalist Society, 82; in Frug-*Revue* controversy, 80, 83; in *Lawrence v. Texas,* 82; on Nesson, 93; and originalism, 127; on Paulin case, 136, 139, 141–43; on *Roe v. Wade,* 81; as solicitor general, 42, 83; on speech codes, 193

Frug, Mary Joe, 79–80
Frug-*Revue* controversy, 78–80, 83–86, 94, 115, 192; Dershowitz on, 98–99; Dershowitz vs. Tribe, 139–41
Furman v. Georgia, 26–27

Gabel, Peter, 17–18
Gandhi, Mahatma, 11
gay rights: and military policy, 171–75, 188–90; queer theory, 173–74
Gerken, Heather, 121, 133, 172–73
Ginsburg, Ruth Bader, 31–32
Glendon, Mary Ann, 128
Goad, Amanda, 189
Goldberg, Rita, 135
Gonzaga Law Review, 74
Gordon, Robert, 25
Gore, Al, 136, 138
grading, 22–23, 125–26
graduation rates, 22
Greenberg, Jack, 32–33
Guinier, Lani, 87, 107–9, 185; "cumulative voting," 108; as "quota queen," 108–9
Gulf War, 176

Halley, Janet, 173–75
Hanson, Jon, 130
Harbus, 164
Harcourt, Bernard, 53, 55, 57
Harlan, John Marshall, 47, 81
Harvard, John, 6
Harvard Business School, 164
Harvard Civil Rights–Civil Liberties Law Review, 160

Harvard Civil Rights Project, 114
Harvard Club, 76
Harvard Crimson, 142, 163, 176
Harvard Journal of Law and
    Public Policy, 166–67
Harvard Law Bulletin, 123, 133
Harvard Law Record, 55, 87,
    94, 104, 165, 168, 182, 187,
    190; anti-Americanism in,
    170; double standard, 131–32
Harvard Law Review, 184; affir-
    mative action at, 23; compe-
    tition in, 23; Frug article,
    79–80; influence of, 26; and
    Ogletree, 73; standards of
    scholarship, 79–80
Harvard Law Revue (parody),
    80, 84–85
Helmsley, Leona, 97
Heymann, Philip, 153, 184
Hill, Anita, 73
history of HLS, 6–29
HLCentral, 3, 4–5
HLS (Harvard Law) Republi-
    cans, 119, 121, 166–67, 176
Holmes, Oliver Wendell, 9, 59,
    100; on First Amendment,
    26; legal realism, 12
homosexuality: *Lawrence v.*
    Texas, 82, 174; military pol-
    icy, 170–75; queer theory, 21,
    173–74; sodomy laws, 82, 174
Horowitz, David, 194
Horwitz, Morton, 19–20, 77, 92,
    101
Huckleberry Finn, 149

ideological indoctrination,
    119–22

influence of Harvard Law, 1–2,
    24, 25, 26–29, 31–32
instruction methods, 10–11, 51
Interracial Intimacies
    (Kennedy), 148–49
Islamic Legal Studies Program,
    170
Israel: Dershowitz on, 97–98;
    Paulin on, 135

Jackson, Jesse, 39, 40, 42, 51
Jewish Law Students Associa-
    tion, 139
Jews, 39; anti-Semitism, 45,
    135–37, 142–43; and Israel,
    97–98
John Paul II, Pope, 128
judicial activism, 19–20, 24,
    26–27, 121; vs. democracy,
    111–12

Kagan, Elena, 183–87, 192; and
    conservative students,
    190–91; in Clinton adminis-
    tration, 183–85, 186; on mili-
    tary recruitment, 188–90;
    praise for, 185–86
Kennedy, Anthony, 31
Kennedy, David, 84
Kennedy, Duncan, 16–19, 20,
    21, 83; on janitors as profes-
    sors, 18–19; "politically cor-
    rect" award, 79–80; "Roll
    Over Beethoven," 17–18
Kennedy, Randall, 37, 42, 98; vs.
    Bell, 37, 98, 152, 153; and
    Camara controversy, 148; on
    Critical Race Theory,
    150–51; and Dershowitz,

152–53; on interracial adoption, 148–49; *Nigger,* 149–50; on reparations, 154; on speech codes, 147–53, 154
Kilson, Martin, 152
King, Martin Luther, Jr., 11, 34, 65, 106
Kissinger, Henry, 41–42
Kraakman, Reinier, 83

Lambda, 171, 189, 190
Langdell, Christopher Columbus, 10
Lat-Crit Theory, 21
Lawrence, Charles, 150, 159–60
Lawrence v. Texas, 82, 174
lawsuits (hiring discrimination), 40–41
Legal Aid Bureau, 66
legal positivism, 11–12
legal realism, 12, 24
liberation theology, 14
Lowell, Abbott Lawrence, 146

"Managing Difficult Conversations" seminars, 105–7
Marshall, Thurgood, 33, 183
Marxism, 13, 62, 76–77; liberation theology, 14; *see also* Critical Legal Studies
Massachusetts Civil Rights Act, 180–81
Matsuda, Mari, 150, 160–61
McCarthyism, 94, 98
McIntyre v. Ohio Elections Commission, 88
Michelman, Frank, 42, 83, 153, 185; and Bell, 111; on civil liberties, 113; criticism of

democracy, 111–13; and Crits, 111–12; on Diversity Committee, 111, 113, 179–81, 187, 191; judicial activism, 111–12, 127; on originalism, 127–28
Michigan Law Review, 17
Mikva, Abner, 183
military recruitment: "don't ask, don't tell," 170–75, 188; Solomon Amendment, 171–73, 174, 188–90; and Vietnam War, 170–71
Miller, Arthur, 24
Minow, Martha, 187
moral relativism, 105–8

NAACP Legal Defense Fund, 33
National Law Journal, 69, 146
natural law theory, 11
Nesson, Charles, 34, 47–56, 84; on affirmative action, 50–51; apologies by, 91; BLSA complaints about, 66–67; drug use, 52, 93; and Ellsberg, 47–48; faculty relations, 51, 52; on First Amendment, 54; helps Camara, 168; in Justice Dept., 47; mock trial idea (Scholl), 53–56, 57; PBS debates, 52; punishment of, 91–93, 99–101, 109, 152, 179, 193; teaching style, 51; Woburn case, 48–50
New Republic, 70
New Yorker, 168
New York Times, 168
New York Times v. Sullivan, 26, 40, 113

Nietzsche, Friedrich, 105
Nigger: The Strange Career of a Troublesome Word (Kennedy), 149–50, 152
Not All Black and White (Edley), 114

O'Connor, Sandra Day, 123
Ogletree, Charles, 42, 51, 72–75, 87, 179; and Angela Davis, 73; and Anita Hill, 73; on Clark, 157; on criminal justice, 74; on reparations, 72–73; reputation, 72; on speech codes, 72, 74–75, 163; tenure controversy, 73, 77, 78
originalism, 112, 127–28
Oxford University, 6–7

Paper Chase, The (film), 10, 28, 105
Parker, Richard, 186
Paulin, Tom, 135–36, 141–43, 164
Pentagon Papers, 47–48
Peterson, Nels, 62, 121, 133, 164–65, 166, 190, 192; and Students for Free Speech, 165, 190, 192
political contributions, 124–25
Pollard, Jonathan, 97
popular culture, 28–29, 49
Posner, Richard, 123
postmodernism, 13; *see also* Critical Legal Studies
"Postmodernist Feminist Legal Manifesto (An Unfinished Draft)" (Frug), 79–80
Pound, Roscoe, 9, 146; legal realism, 12

prestige of HLS, 1–2, 9
Princeton University, 69, 71
Property class, 120
publicity, 106–7, 179, 192

queer theory, 21, 173–74

Rabinowitz, Dorothy, 106–7
racial gerrymandering, 121–22
racial issues, 4–5, 44–45, 62–63, 65–67; and double standards, 143–44; and free speech, 74–75, 115–16, 163; interracial adoption, 148–49; legal scholarship on, 21–22, 35–37, 72–74, 150–51, 159–61; "racial harassment" code, 87–89, 153, 155; self-segregation, 162–63; *see also* affirmative action; Black Law Students Association; speech codes
Rakoff, Todd, 54, 63, 68, 86, 87, 145; on Nesson, 91–92; on Rosenberg, 94
Rawls, John, 61
Reagan, Ronald, 81
Record, The. See Harvard Law Record
Regents of the University of California v. Bakke, 23
Rehnquist, William, 36, 123
Reich, Robert, 60
reparations, 72–73, 154
Reversal of Fortune (Dershowitz), 97
Reynolds, Gerald, 182–83
Reynolds, William Bradford, 138

Richardson, Suzanne, 54, 68, 86
Roe v. Wade, 81, 110
Rosenberg, David, 57–63, 91;
 abrasiveness, 57–58, 62; on
 academic freedom & civil
 liberties, 75, 58–59, 60–61; on
 class-action suits, 59; complaints about, 63, 66–67; as
 "conservative," 61; on Critical Legal Studies, 60–63,
 93–94; punishment of, 93–96,
 100–1, 109, 152, 179, 193;
 racial issues, 62–63; respect
 for, 58
Rousseau, Jean-Jacques, 13
Royall, Isaac, 7
Rudenstein, Neil, 84, 111

Sacco, Nicola, 146
Scalia, Antonin, 28, 31, 112, 123,
 195; originalism, 127
Schlichtmann, Jan, 48–50
Scholl, Matthias: BLSA complaints about, 66–68; con-
 fesses to e-mails, 53–55; on
 free speech rights, 55; "gcrocodile" e-mails, 44–45; and
 mock trial, 54, 91; as outsider, 166; punishment of,
 165, 179; reprimand of,
 87–88; shunning of, 165–66
Schwartz, Lacey, 67, 106
sensitivity training, 67; for faculty, 107, 109; "Difficult
 Conversations," 105–7, 182
September 11 attacks, 169–70,
 173
sexual harassment, 59, 94, 115,
 192; vs. sexism, 155

Shadow University, The (Silverglate), 85
Sharpton, Al, 71
Shelley v. Kraemer, 4
Silverglate, Harvey, 181, 196;
 and FIRE, 58, 165; on Frug-
 Revue controversy, 84, 85, 86,
 88; on Nesson, 100–1; on
 Rosenberg, 58, 60–61, 100–1;
 on sensitivity training, 106–7;
 on speech codes, 94, 105,
 153–54, 157, 162, 192
Simpson, F. Michelle, 5, 43–44,
 45, 53, 54, 61
Singer, Joseph, 130–31
Skinner, Walter, Jay, 49–50
Skrmetti, Jonathan, 122, 124,
 133, 166
slavery: emancipation, 74–75;
 reparations for, 72–73, 154
Socratic method, 10–11, 95, 105
Solomon Amendment, 171–73,
 174, 188–90; lawsuit against,
 189
Souter, David, 31
Specter, Arlen, 73
speech codes: BLSA demand,
 67, 86–87, 147, 151, 152,
 154–55, 162, 187; in Canada,
 194; Clark's plans, 87, 89, 94,
 104–5; conservative opposition, 117, 131, 163–65,
 190–91; court opposition,
 145, 161–62; de facto, 124;
 Dershowitz on, 99–100, 115,
 145–46, 147, 152–53, 154–55;
 Diversity Committee on,
 115–16, 145, 147, 150–55; in
 France, 193–94; and military

speech codes (cont.)
recruitment, 190; Office for
Civil Rights on, 182–83;
Ogletree on, 74–75; at private institution, 145, 181;
publicity on, 94, 179, 192;
"racial harassment policy,"
87–89; scholarly basis for,
74–75, 159–62; and sexual
harassment, 94; at U. of
Michigan, 161; at U. of Wisconsin, 161–62; waning support for, 179–83, 187, 190,
191–96
Stanford Law Review, 17, 40
Stewart, Potter, 137
Story, Joseph, 8–9
Students for Free Speech, 165,
190, 192
Summers, Lawrence, 136,
181–82, 183, 192; and Cornel
West, 71; dean selection, 183,
185–6

tenure: battles over, 34, 38,
40–41, 60, 73, 77, 78, 187;
failure of, 101
Theory of Justice, A (Rawls), 61
Thernstrom, Abigail, 128–29
Thernstrom, Stephan, 128–30,
144; on "McCarthyism of the
left," 129
Thomas, Clarence, 37–38, 112;
confirmation hearings, 73;
originalism, 127
Timmons, Bruce, 19
Tocqueville, Alexis de, 115
Toobin, Jeffrey, 168
Torts class, 119–20

*Transformation of American
Law, The* (Horwitz), 19
Tribe, Laurence, 24, 185; on
Bork, 137; in California
gubernatorial recall, 138; on
Clinton impeachment, 138;
and Dershowitz, 139–41;
earnings, 141; on Frug-*Revue*
controversy, 139–41; Gore
election challenge, 136, 138;
and Paulin case, 136. 139,
141–44; reputation, 137–38;
Supreme Court ambitions,
136, 137–38; in Supreme
Court argument, 24, 27
Trubek, David, 77
Turow, Scott, 10
Tyson, Mike, 97

Unger, Roberto, 14–16, 157
Unitarians, 118–19
United Nations World Confer-
ence against Racism, 72
University of Michigan, 114, 161
University of Oregon School of
Law, 34
University of Wisconsin, 161
U.S. Air Force, 171
U.S. Constitution: Civil War
Amendments, 75; and judi-
cial activism, 112; Second
Amendment, 99; *see also*
First Amendment; U.S.
Supreme Court
U.S. Court of Appeals, D.C.
Circuit, 183, 184
U.S. Court of Appeals, Ninth
Circuit, 27, 138
U.S. Department of Defense, 189

U.S. Department of Education: Office for Civil Rights, 182–83

U.S. Department of Justice: Civil Rights Division, 33, 47, 107

U.S. Supreme Court, 8, 9, 136, 180–81; affirmative action cases (2003), 114; on anonymous speech, 88, 165; *Bakke,* 23; *Bush v. Gore,* 27, 99, 136, 138; *Chaplinsky v. New Hampshire,* 161–62; clerks, 28; *Furman v. Georgia,* 26–27; Harvard alumni on, 31–32; Harvard influence on, 24, 26–27, 195–96; judicial activism on, 20; *Lawrence v. Texas,* 82, 174; *McIntyre v. Ohio Elections Commission,* 88; *New York Times v. Sullivan,* 26; originalism, 127; on racial gerrymandering, 122; *Virginia v. Black,* 180

Vanity Fair, 141
Vanzetti, Bartolomeo, 146
Vietnam War, 65, 87; recruiters banned, 170–71
Virginia v. Black, 180
Vogel, Frank, 170
von Bulow, Claus, 96–97
Vorenberg, James, 32–33, 77, 159

Wall Street Journal, 19, 43, 94, 106–7, 124, 157
war protests, 65, 170, 176–77
Warren, Earl, 19–20, 24, 113, 127

Warren, Edward H. "Bull," 9, 22, 105
Warren, Elizabeth, 51
Wells, Tom, 48
West, Cornel, 69–72, 148; and Christianity, 69, 70; ego, 69–70; intellectual scorn for, 70–71; leaves for Princeton, 71; Marxism, 69, 70; rap CD, 71; on separatism, 162; vs. Summers, 71; as University Professor, 69
White v. Crook, 47
Wieseltier, Leon, 70–71
William and Mary College, 7
women on faculty, 38, 39–41, 186–87
"Words That Wound" (Delgado), 160
World Trade Center, 169–70

Yale Law Journal, 22